CONSTITUTIONAL CONCERNS

Writings on Law and Life

CONSTITUTIONAL CONCERNS

Writings on Law and Life

KALEESWARAM RAJ

Tulika Books

Published by
Tulika Books
44 (first floor), Shahpur Jat, New Delhi 110 049, India
www.tulikabooks.in

First published in India in 2022

ISBN: 978-81-950559-8-2 (hardback)

Contents

Foreword

TWO INALIENABLE FEATURES of democracy are the adherence to the rule of law and equal protection of laws to all citizens and also to subjects who are not even citizens.

In a democracy, where a written Constitution exists as the supreme law regulating the conduct of the state in its various branches, the judiciary is entrusted with the responsibility of ensuring that the Rule of Law, prevails and the governance of the country is carried on in accordance with the Constitution and the laws made thereunder – provided, of course, that the laws are consistent with the Constitution.

How faithful the various branches of governance are at a given point of time to the Constitution is a matter of opinion. But surely, there are some time-tested parameters by which such an assessment is to be made and opinion formed.

The opinion of the masses is mostly moulded by propaganda. However, the judiciary is expected to rest its opinions and conclusions on surer foundations.

An assessment of the working of the democracy for the last few years with specific reference to the functioning of the judicial branch is the subject matter of this book. Naturally, such an exercise can be undertaken by members of the legal fraternity more effectively because they are trained in the discipline of law.

I was in the law college when Mrs Indira Gandhi's Emergency was proclaimed. Soon thereafter, I joined the Bar. I must recall with satisfaction, members of the legal profession were seriously debating the legality of not only the proclamation, but also the excesses of the administrative actions in an atmosphere where the fundamental rights of the citizens were kept in suspension. Even in those days, there was a strong section of the Bar which supported the Emergency, not to mention the bench and the *ADM Jabalpur* case (1976).

Forty-five years later, I am afraid that the Indian Bar has largely abandoned the critical evaluation of the working of democracy and the law declared by the constitutional courts on many important questions which impact civil society greatly, barring a few exceptions like Kaleeswaram Raj.

Whether one agrees with them or not, the views of Kaleeswaram Raj are clear. His mind is focused on the core principles of democracy. He is bold and candid.

In an age when public opinion is moulded by Facebook and Twitter, not many perhaps have time for evaluation of the working of various institutions designed to promote the rule of law and protect democracy.

The survival of any democracy depends upon the vigilance of its citizens. All vigilant citizens are not always articulate, and, therefore, their ability to influence the opinions of fellow citizens is limited.

It is the more articulate citizens like Kaleeswaram Raj who take the trouble to enlighten the civil society by publishing the fruits of their hard work, hoping to serve the country and its citizens. It is for the civil society to decide whether to benefit or not from the wisdom of such people.

I congratulate Mr Kaleeswaram Raj for his endeavours.

Hyderabad   JUSTICE J. CHELAMESWAR
                                               Judge (Retd), Supreme Court of India

Preface and Acknowledgements

M Y JOURNEY FROM the mofussil courts in north Kerala to the country's top court was motivated more by curiosity than by ambition. To watch the political developments with a legal eye and the legal developments with a political eye is a task that every constitutional lawyer must genuinely undertake. It is an amazing yet challenging experience. The articles on certain events in law and society were written as part of this process of self-education and public education.

My earlier work, *Rethinking Judicial Reforms: Reflections on Indian Legal System*, was first published in 2017 by LexisNexis (Universal). But the metamorphosis that the country's legal system has undergone since then needs political analysis with a sense of contemporariness. The articles in this book, which were initially carried by the newspapers, *The New Indian Express, The Hindu, The Telegraph, Deccan Herald,* and the journal *Frontline*, try to address the pathological issues concerning the country's legal landscape in recent years. The *constitutional concerns* that arose during the tough times are also dreams in disguise – dreams that we might share.

I wish to express my sincere thanks to the editors of *The New Indian Express, The Hindu, The Telegraph, Deccan Herald* and *Frontline* for publishing the pieces originally, and for facilitating a discourse on the topics. It needed further editorial work to compile the articles in the present form. It is the proactive support from my publisher that materialized this project. I wish to place on record my immense gratitude to Tulika Books and Ms Indira Chandrasekhar, its founder and managing editor. Timely and critical suggestions from Haobam Basantarani helped me immensely in finalizing the book. Uttara Vijayakumar and Niyatha Rajeev who assisted in proof corrections also deserve appreciation.

Thanks are also due to my wife Sudha, for her endurance and involvement in finalizing the text of the articles. My daughter Thulasi and son-in-law Bastian Steuwer were of great help in the same process. It is in a way a by-product of the peace and happiness that my family always gave me (which, perhaps, I could not pay in return).

I am beholden to Sashi Kumar, pioneer of modern journalism in India, for encouraging my juristic pursuits in various ways. My friend K. Gopakumar emotionally and intellectually shared many of my concerns. That brought a lot of comfort in my life.

Also, I am indebted to my junior colleagues Varun C. Vijay and others for their wholehearted efforts in my litigation firm, which provided me the time and space to think and write. Their continuing solidarity is unforgettable.

New Delhi   KALEESWARAM RAJ

Introduction

D EMOCRACIES ARE IN danger. They are receding across the world with just a few instances of revival, as happened in the US with the defeat of Donald Trump. And, as many apprehend, authoritarianism prevails in many nations in various forms. The point is to understand the present context better and to exercise our political duty to ensure a better world with a better polity, which is a difficult task.

The constitutional scholar Tarunabh Khaitan says that in several democracies executive aggrandizement is 'incremental and systemic'; it 'uses democratic rhetoric, and is effected by the fusion of the ruling party and the state'.[1] He also carefully explains how this applies in the Indian context.[2] Though he says that the executive is 'arguably the most dangerous branch',[3] it is significant to understand the interplay of the formal and informal branches of governance and the governed in the process of democratic destabilization. Alexander Hamilton conceived the judiciary as the 'least dangerous branch'.[4] This may require a contextual and realistic understanding in the contemporary world. In many instances, the executive actions of de-constitutionalization are abetted or facilitated by the judiciary, by a process of 'abusive judicial review', as David Landau and Rosalind Dixon have remarkably put it.[5]

The Indian situation is peculiar in many respects. Very often, the executive relies on legislative onslaughts like the Citizenship Amendment Act, in support of its action. When opponents of the regime are arrested and detained under various draconian provisions, jail becomes the rule and the new normal for political dissent. Laws work together with the executive,

---

[1] Tarunabh Khaitan, 'Executive Aggrandizement in Established Democracies: A Crisis of Liberal Democratic Constitutionalism', *International Journal of Constitutional Law*, 2019.

[2] Tarunabh Khaitan, 'Killing a Constitution with a Thousand Cuts: Executive Aggrandizement and Party State Fusion in India', *Law and Ethics of Human Rights*, 2019.

[3] Khaitan, 'Executive Aggrandizement in Established Democracies'.

[4] Alexander Hamilton, 'Federalist No. 78', *The Federalist Papers*, United States of America, 1788.

[5] David Landau and Rosalind Dixon, 'Abusive Judicial Review: Courts Against Democracy', *UC Davis Law Review*, vol. 53, 2020. For an illustrative instance, see chapter 5.

and the judiciary mostly remains a passive spectator. Thus, one finds a complex interplay of various actors in the saga of democratic erosion. The absolutism and centrism attached to the dispensation has narrowed the space for dialogue, discourse and introspection. There is no democracy when the nation is substantially muted.

Self-correction needs a democratic attitude, especially during the critical times of the pandemic. The BBC telecast the depositions of Dominic Cummings, the former chief advisor to Prime Minister Boris Johnson, exposing the UK government's mistakes in handling the Covid-19 contagion which led to thousands of deaths. On the contrary, one found several Indian authorities in denial mode, despite casualties across the country for want of oxygen, treatment or vaccine.

Lack of planning and strategies in the health care system led to countless human tragedies during the Covid-19 pandemic in India. The systemic failure abetted by ideological timidity of the regime was clear. The public had to pay a heavy cost for the institutional setback. The health crisis was also a constitutional and political crisis. This situation underlines the pressing need for democratic governance in the real sense of the phrase. The institutional behaviour needs careful study that transcends the immediate. Often, public intellectuals fail in meeting this challenge. We lose the dynamism of discourse and the honesty to see ourselves.

Steven Levitsky and Daniel Ziblatt have explained the nature of democratic crisis in their seminal work.[6] But they fail to see the damage that the polity in India suffered in the ongoing global trend. The authors say that along with few other countries, Indian democracy 'remained intact through 2017'. This erroneous judgment cannot sustain. The new regime under the Bharatiya Janata Party (BJP), with an ideological shift, started to dismantle the constitutional institutions in India right from 2014. Growing instances of vigilantism, communal divide, use of sedition law and other laws against dissenters, lack of discourse in matters of governance in the Cabinet or in the Parliament, threat to the institutions including the public universities, and many other anti-democratic tendencies were accelerated during this period. Most of them had the direct or indirect involvement of the state. Democracy in India has started to disintegrate since then.[7]

---

[6] Steven Levitsky and Daniel Ziblatt, *How Democracies Die*, Penguin Books, 2018.
[7] During the National Emergency (1975–77) also, the country's democracy had suffered severely.

An unfair state is also the result of a populace that chooses to embrace a false notion of safety under an autocracy. Whether the public at large is concerned with truth, freedom, equality and dignity is a crucial question in any discourse on democracy. The moral psychology of the citizen is an important factor. The people impact the regime, and the regime impacts the people. The media, including social media, determine public opinion in strange and often undesirable ways.

We also need public intellectuals of a different brand to carry out the laborious yet inescapable task of looking at what is happening around us. In his classic work *Representation of the Intellectual*, Edward W. Said analysed various limiting factors which public intellectuals might face in questioning power.[8] In the era of elected autocracies, mere intellectual autonomy, or generic wisdom, or moral authority of the critic, might not be adequate to understand the threats to democracy. It also needs to rely on the theoretical devices of the Constitution to watch its own institutions and their predicament. This task is not easy in a post-truth world. We have to get back to our systemic devices to know the systemic debacles. Individuals have influence, but only when the institutions are set right.

Therefore, we must think in terms of a vigilant examination of contemporary events with reference to their impact on politics. This analysis can help us understand the trend of elected authoritarianism in India and the lessons that follow.

This collection of articles, which originally appeared as separate pieces, tries to make a contextual analysis of certain constitutional moments in India in the most recent times, from a lawyer's point of view.

The book is divided into five parts. Part One is on laws, Part Two on the courts, Part Three on freedom, Part Four on politics and Part Five on life. The parts are clearly interlinked and might overlap with one another. The chapters were written as articles in newspapers or periodicals during 2018–21, when India's democracy was struggling. The country has suffered tremendous setbacks to her constitutionalism. The impact of these developments on democracy and governance must be analysed to think about a rescue

---

[8] Edward W. Said, *Representations of the Intellectual: The 1993 Reith Lectures*, New York: Vintage Books, 1996.

operation. The world's largest democracy, as we were, needs to revamp not only its institutions, but attitudes as well. For this, legal and constitutional tools must be applied contextually and imaginatively.

The first four chapters in the first part try to take stock of a few parliamentary legislations of recent origin. Students of law are conversant with laws becoming unconstitutional on certain established grounds like breaching fundamental rights or lacking legislative competence. But the recent legislative trends in India indicate a deliberate attempt to overturn the very constitutional scheme. This shows a paradigm shift in the process of law-making, calling for strong political opposition rooted in the fundamental law of the country. The fight against majoritarianism is no longer an in-house matter.

The court as an institution needs to be constantly watched and critiqued at a time when the distinction between legal issues and political issues is blurred. Chapters 5 to 18 contained in Part Two of the book carry out this task. They deal with the authority, methodology, language and attitude of the courts in various contexts.

The imprisonment of political prisoners in India is a serious issue warranting introspective analysis. The culpability of the state and those who run it is not to be seen as an isolated or distinct feature. The attitude of the courts, the media and the people have a determining role in making and perpetuating the glaringly unjust incarcerations that epitomize the clutches of India's elected autocracy. Chapters 19 to 24 in Part Three look at the questions of freedom that have arisen in different contexts.

It was the political challenge to the farm laws rather than the legal challenge that ultimately compelled the Modi-2 regime to repeal them. This episode emphasizes the relevance of people's movements. The people at large and their peaceful protests need to be understood in the constitutional sense, to see how far it is an effective device for protecting the basic political document that the nation created for the people. Law's morality always reflects the political morality.

Governance in a constitutional democracy cannot be a solo show. It is a collective and purposive activity of individuals facilitated by institutions. Those at the helm of affairs are expected to behave constitutionally. Part Four of the book, consisting of chapters 25 to 39, addresses the issues of mass movements, electoral process, governance, etc. It is hoped that these sketches will indicate the trajectory of Indian democracy in contemporary India, which in turn will help us to think about reconstitutionalizing the country, which alone help us to save ourselves.

'Life of the law has not been logic. It has been experience', said Oliver Wendell Holmes, Jr.[9] Laws dealing with life also require an empirical analysis. Chapters 40 to 43 in Part Five are on questions of life that emerged in different specific situations. American theologian Reinhold Niebuhr famously said that man's capacity for justice makes democracy possible, but his inclination to injustice makes it necessary.[10] For us, it is both possible and necessary, and this book, I feel, rests on this sense of exigency.

---

[9] https://www.britannica.com/biography/Oliver-Wendell-Holmes-Jr/The-Common-Law, accessed 9 January 2021.

[10] https://www.oxfordreference.com/view/10.1093/acref/9780191843730.001.0001/q-oro-ed5-00007882, accessed 9 January 2021.

PART ONE

ON LAWS

1. When Laws Subvert the Constitution

Legislations are often unconstitutional and courts declare them so. But laws can also be 'anti-constitutional', in the sense that they can also subvert the Constitution. Such laws pose a formal and significant threat to democracy, especially when enacted without deliberations inside or outside the Parliament. People's protests alone might remain as an effective check, as demonstrated by the effective repeal of the farm laws in India in 2021.

CONSTITUTIONAL DEMOCRACY fundamentally differs from conventional democracy. Though majority matters in both, in the former, the opinion of the majority is subjected to constitutional limitations. In a way, one of the main objects of modern constitutions is to protect nations from any majoritarian onslaught. This, in a way, is an ethical check. It is the majority that speaks through their representatives in the legislatures. Legislation should pass the constitutional muster.

POLITICS OF LEGISLATION

A legislation reflects an ideology, an attitude and an approach. In India, between 1952 and 1984, governments at the centre enjoyed a clear majority. During this period, the country saw a series of enactments, including progressive ones that led to the nationalization of banks and abolition of the privy purse. Politics has never remained static in the country. The same has been the situation regarding the vision and philosophy of political parties. The same political party that attempted certain radical reforms under the label of Nehruvian socialism attempted to suspend the personal and political freedoms of citizens during the National Emergency (1975–77). Again, ironically yet rightly, the very same political party is now pleading for freedoms guaranteed by the Constitution. The present oppressor used to be a major partner of the Janata coalition against the Indira Gandhi regime: namely the Bharatiya Janata Party (BJP), which was then the Jana Sangh.

One finds that there was a qualitative change in legislative attitudes during the short period of the Congress party-led United Progressive Alliance (UPA) government, from 2004 to 2014. Welfare and progressive laws such as the Mahatma Gandhi National Rural Employment Guarantee Act, 2005; the Traditional Forest Dwellers (Recognition of Forest Rights) Act, 2006;

the Right to Education Act, 2009; the Right to Fair Compensation and Transparency in Land Acquisition, Rehabilitation and Resettlement Act, 2013; the Right to Information Act, 2005; the National Food Security Act, 2013; and the Street Vendors (Protection of Livelihood and Regulation of Street Vending) Act, 2014 – all were promulgated during the UPA period. Make no mistake, even at that time the centre had tried to suppress criticism and crush public protest by invoking draconian laws. Nevertheless, there were egalitarian streams in the process of law-making as reflected in the pieces of legislation mentioned above. Also, there was a democratic space to protest, agitate and articulate against the follies of power, which in turn placed the UPA period relatively at a higher scale of deliberative democracy.

Many of the major laws enacted under the present BJP-led NDA (National Democratic Alliance) regime, on the other hand, show a clear ideological shift with an aggressive Hindutva agenda blended with a capitalist ethos. They are centrist and absolutist in terms of power, and divisive and destructive in terms of societal interest.

After 1984 – when the Congress swept to power in the parliamentary election held after the assassination of Indira Gandhi – it was only in 2014, with the BJP coming to power, that single-party dominance was resurrected at the centre, accompanied by a fundamental change in ideology. It differed from the single-party rule and from the flexible and federal politics of the coalition regimes of earlier decades. This shift was not only due to majoritarianism *per se*, but also due to doctrinal reasons that can have devastating consequences.

K.K. Kailash of the Department of Political Science, University of Hyderabad, says: 'Both the Congress and the BJP are closet centralizers and reluctant federalists, with one significant difference. While both justify centralization in the name of economic development and national unity and integrity, for the BJP there is also an ethnic, religious or cultural dimension at play'.[1] Kailash rightly indicates that the two vary drastically in their approach to pluralism. But on a closer examination, one finds that the difference between them is not peripheral or external. It is extremely distinct inasmuch as the dispensation at the centre after 2014 does not believe in the ethos of the Constitution or its institutions. Hindutva forces strengthen its regime and weaken its opponents with a well-designed project started almost a century ago, and, in the process, great damage has been caused to constitutional praxis

[1] K.K. Kailash, '"One Nation", New India and the Hollowing Out of the Federal Idea', February 2021, https://www.theindiaforum.in/article/one-nation-new-india-and-hollowing-out-federal-idea, accessed on 25 November 2021.

in India. The damage caused to institutions ranging from the Cabinet to the courts to Parliament, and to informal institutions such as the media, has been enormous and probably irreparable in the near future.

An examination of the pieces of legislation brought in by the NDA reveals a systematic, conscious and constant effort to 'deconstitutionalize' the country. Many such enactments were manifestations of far-right politics rooted in Hindutva ideology and crony capitalism. The statute on instant triple talaq[2] – The Muslim Women (Protection of Rights on Marriage) Act, 2019 – was ostensibly partisan. It targeted a particular community. The fallacy of the law was self-evident. It tried to 'invalidate' triple talaq, which was already invalidated by the Supreme Court in *Shayara Bano v. Union of India* (2017)[3] by way of a majority judgment. By criminalizing a void action, the 2019 Act, in certain situations, even tried to prevent divorced women from getting maintenance from their former husbands, who could be incarcerated for the offence of triple talaq as defined, for a period of up to three years and pay a fine, as per Section 4 of the Act. It also had the effect of instigating husbands to desert their wives without leaving a formal proof of divorce, in order to escape the clutches of the law. Thus the law did not even serve Muslim women's interest, despite its populist gestures. Although the law was unimaginative and 'foolish' in the legal sense, it clearly had a shrewd political content that subserved the centre's agenda. The Citizenship (Amendment) Act, 2019[4] also clearly attempts to segregate people on communal and religious lines. They are clearly antithetical to the equality clauses in the Constitution. They negate the preambular notions of dignity and fraternity.

---

[2] *Talaq-e-biddat* among Muslims is an instantaneous and irrevocable divorce, which is so defined in the statute as well. Its effect on the civil and personal rights of the parties could be drastic and immediate.

[3] In this case ([2017] 9 SCC 1), the petitioner Shayara Bano challenged the action of her husband pronouncing instantaneous triple talaq and divorcing her. The top court considered the case along with a few others, and set aside the practice of triple talaq by a majority of 3:2.

[4] According to the amendment made to Section 2 of the Citizenship Act, 1955, only persons belonging to Hindu, Sikh, Buddhist, Jain, Parsi or Christian communities from Afghanistan, Bangladesh or Pakistan will not be treated as illegal migrants. This benefit is not extended to Muslim migrants from these countries. Thus, persons are classified based on their religion. A similar disparity is reflected in certain other parts of the enactment. For citizenship by naturalization, these communities require only a minimum of five years as aggregate period of residence or service in India. For a Muslim, the minimum period for this purpose is eleven years. The Third Schedule of the Act is amended this way.

The state laws on 'love jihad'[5] also imagine something non-existent, namely, planned and targeted conversion for the purpose of marriage so as to boost religious or even fanatic interest. On 1 April 2021, the Gujarat Assembly passed the ironically named Freedom of Religion Act, 2003, an amendment bill criminalizing 'love jihad'. The offences enumerated are non-bailable. Forcible conversion through marriage or allurement can lead to imprisonment for a term of three to ten years and a fine of up to Rs 5 lakh. The way in which similar laws are designed and invoked in Uttar Pradesh, Madhya Pradesh, Uttarakhand and Himachal Pradesh tells a disheartening saga of torturing young couples for their personal relations and choices. For political gain, the dispensation always tries to create and perpetuate a communally divided society. Also, it intrudes upon individual decisions and personal affairs. This trend is unprecedented in the legislative history of the country.

The abrogation of the special status of Kashmir in August 2019 has negated the historical reasons behind Article 370,[6] which the original Constitution tried to understand and accept. The three contentious farm laws passed in 2020 – The Farmers' Produce Trade and Commerce (Promotion and Facilitation) Act, the Farmers (Empowerment and Protection) Agreement on Price Assurance and Farm Services Act, the Essential Commodities (Amendment) Act – too were non-discursive, centrist and pro-capitalist, on the face of it. They threatened not just the farmers and their dignity but the very food security in the country by abolishing the conventional network created by the Food Corporation of India. Decisions in favour of the massive sale of public properties ranging from coal mines to airports were all supported by majoritarianism at the centre. The Cabinet too, like the Parliament, perpetually and intentionally avoided discourse. Obedience and unilateralism are the hallmark of centrist forces. When the farm laws were repealed towards the end of 2021, it was a triumph for constitutionalism in India too, which the farmers were able to uphold.

---

[5] The term 'love jihad', in common parlance, denotes a belief that Muslim men woo Hindu women in order to marry them in a clandestine way so as fulfil an agenda to convert them to Islam. This 'theory' has, however, no rational or empirical basis.

[6] Special status was given to the then state of Jammu and Kashmir based on the terms of the Instrument of Accession. This ensured relatively better autonomy for the state by limiting the legislative power of the Parliament.

Undoing Electoral Democracy

The centre's legislative attempt by way of introducing in the Lok Sabha, on 15 March 2021, the Government of National Capital Territory of Delhi (Amendment) Bill, 2021, was in continuation with its project to subvert the tenets of federalism. But more significantly, it contains an attack on the country's electoral democracy. In *Government of NCT of Delhi v. Union of India and Ors.* (2018),[7] a constitution bench of the Supreme Court clarified in its judgment on 4 July 2018, that the 'Lieutenant Governor [of Delhi] is an administrative head in the limited sense' and that 'he is bound by the aid and advice of the NCT [National Capital Territory] government in areas other than those exempted'. The court further said that 'if a well-deliberated legitimate decision of the council of ministers is not given effect due to an attitude to differ on the part of the Lieutenant Governor, then the concept of collective responsibility would stand negated'. This was how the court interpreted the purport of Article 239AA of the Constitution, inserted by the Constitution 69th Amendment Act, 1991 with effect from 1 February 1992.[8] Clearly, the very purpose of the special status given to Delhi, as clarified by the court, was to ensure democratic governance based on the people's mandate as reflected in the Assembly. The new legislation will annihilate even the limited autonomy granted to Delhi. In the matter of land, police and public order, the Delhi government did not have power even otherwise. With the amendment, the Lieutenant Governor literally and substantially becomes the 'Government of Delhi'. According to the new provisions, on all matters specified by the Lieutenant Governor, his opinion should be sought and obtained by the Cabinet. This will seriously impair the tenets of cooperative and competitive federalism. On the one hand, it reduces the scope for governance by the elected Cabinet in Delhi, which in turn diminishes its capacity to meaningfully assert itself with the centre and other states by maintaining a healthy and dignified relationship. On the other hand, the new law reduces the state's autonomy and its potential to develop itself by reformative strategies. Competitive federalism, in the correct and positive sense, also underlines this potential, which if taken away, will make the Assembly election meaningless.

---

[7] (2018) 8 SCC 501.

[8] Article 239AA contemplates a legislative assembly for the National Capital Territory of Delhi. Even though the Parliament has legislative power over Delhi, the Article recognizes the identity of the Legislative Assembly and its power to make laws for the whole or any part of the territory, subject to certain conditions.

In recent times, even without any particular legislative measure, Governors from West Bengal to Puducherry, as nominees of the centre, have meddled with the day-to-day decisions of elected governments. In the normal course, in full-fledged states, Governors are only titular heads. As Dr B.R. Ambedkar said during the Constituent Assembly debates, 'The Governor under the Constitution has no functions which he can discharge by himself . . . [and he] is bound to accept the advice of the Ministry.' This principle, which was eloquently reiterated by the constitution bench of the Supreme Court in *Shamsher Singh v. State of Punjab* (1974),[9] should apply to Delhi also, especially after the insertion of Article 239AA of the Constitution in 1991. V.S. Ramadevi, former Chief Election Commissioner and former Governor of Karnataka, once quoted Professor R. Venkata Rao to explain the 'power' of the Governor: 'Useless when inert and dangerous when active.' In a different context, the amendment to the Government of National Capital Territory of Delhi Act, 1991 makes it democratically dangerous, for, practically, the elected government cannot do anything without the nod of the Governor.

FALSE CLAIMS AND OBLIQUE MOTIVES

The historical, geographical or administrative specificities of Delhi cannot take away the democratic value and relevance of an elected government there. The amendment to the Delhi statute nullified the top court's verdict which, *inter alia*, read the relevant articles of the Constitution, i.e. Article 239AA (3)(a) and Article 239AA (4) conjointly, and said that 'the executive power of the Government of NCT of Delhi is coextensive with the legislative power of the Delhi Legislative Assembly' and that 'the Constitution confers executive power on the Council of Ministers over all those subjects in respect of which the Delhi Legislative Assembly has the legislative power'. This principle is now substituted by way of a statutory (not constitutional) amendment. The third paragraph of the statement of objects beneath the bill unconvincingly and artificially relied on the Supreme Court's judgments of 4

---

[9] In this case ([1974] 2 SCC 831), a subordinate judge in Punjab who was terminated from service while on probation assailed the action as one by the Chief Minister without the Governor's approval. It was also contended that the Governor was supposed to exercise personal discretion in such matters. This contention was rejected by the court saying that the Governor, in such matters, can only act under the aid and advice of the Cabinet as provided under Article 163 of the Constitution. However, on other grounds, the termination was set aside.

July 2018 and 14 February 2019, and said that the new amendment was to 'give effect to the interpretation made by the Hon. Supreme Court', whereas what happens is a clear negation of what the court said in its pronouncement in 2018. Again, in the fourth paragraph of the statement the claim is that the bill 'will promote harmonious relations between the legislature and the executive, and further define the responsibilities of the elected government and the Lieutenant Governor, in line with the constitutional scheme of governance of National Capital Territory of Delhi, as interpreted by the Hon. Supreme Court'. Not only is this untrue, it is also opposite to the truth. The Chief Minister of Delhi, Arvind Kejriwal, has already protested against the legislation by taking the issue to the streets, an event which no longer has the characteristics of 'harmonious relation' that the text of the law claimed to attain. This inversion of truth, that too in a piece of statute, is alarming. False claims and oblique motives in the process of legislation are grey areas for any student of constitutional law, as the law presumes that a statute made by the legislature is valid, and a legislation cannot be vitiated by malice.

The Supreme Court, in *K. Nagaraj and Ors. v. State of Andhra Pradesh and Ors.* (1985),[10] held that in the matter of legislative power 'the argument of mala fides is misconceived', and that 'the legislature as a body cannot be accused of having passed a law for an extraneous purpose'. This position was reiterated in *Gurudevadatta v. State of Maharashtra* (2001)[11] and most recently in *Manish Kumar v. Union of India* (2021).[12] As we shall see more specifically in the next chapter, this conventional principle does not appear to be sensible in India's new legislative or political landscape. Constitutional principles are feasible only when there is a political climate capable of sustaining constitutionalism.

A few other recent legislative ventures have the common characteristics of negating one or other basic feature of the Constitution. The Amendment to the Juvenile Justice (Care and Protection of Children) Act, 2015, vests the executive magistrates with judicial powers in the matter of adoption of children. This nullifies the idea of separation of power at the most personal and grassroot level. There was turmoil and protests in the Bihar Assembly when it passed the Special Armed Police Bill, 2021, on 23 March 2021. The new law grants the Bihar Military Police (BMP) the power of the Central Industrial Security Force (CISF) to conduct search and arrest without a warrant issued

[10] (1985) 1 SCC 523.
[11] (2001) 4 SCC 534.
[12] (2021) 5 SCC 1.

by a competent court. The power and discretion of the judiciary are curtailed since the court cannot take cognizance when there are accusations against a special armed police officer, unless there is an enabling report prepared with the previous sanction of the government. The new Act extends the Union government's police power to the state. A police state is thus created by the state legislature, presumably at the behest of the centre.

Such moves are accelerated in a situation where the judiciary fails to scan the laws and verify their constitutionality fairly, vigilantly and objectively. The rulers often ask the protesters to challenge the laws in court, as happened in the case of the farm laws. Legislations need public scrutiny. The ultimate solution lies with people's peaceful movements. Solidarity against inhuman and unconstitutional laws is a democratic imperative in present-day India. As memorably stated by Thomas Jefferson, 'When injustice becomes law, resistance becomes duty.' We cannot afford to ignore the 'argumentative Indians'. Legislation is too important to be left to legislators alone.

Frontline, 23 April 2021, https://frontline.thehindu.com/cover-story/when-laws-subvert-the-constitution-need-for-movement-against-anti-constitutional-laws/article34244247.ece.

2. A Case of Unprincipled Criminalization

In chapter 1, instances are cited of legislations themselves attacking the Constitution. This article focuses on one such law, the 'triple talaq' law, which is about targeted criminalization. It was first written while the bill was being designed, before it became an Act, and has since been updated.

IN AN ESSAY published in the *Washington University Law Review* (1979), Martin R. Gardner posed a significant question: can an 'illicit legislative motivation' be 'a sufficient condition for unconstitutionality'?[1] He explored this 'muddled area' in the context of religious motivation under the establishment clause of the US Constitution, and said that 'the claim that religious motivation justifies invalidation is controversial and largely conjectured'. He however identified 'significant sectarian motivation' without a 'secular purpose' as a ground for invalidation of the law.

The content of the Muslim Women (Protection of Rights on Marriage) Act (2019) clearly reflects a sectarian overtone that attempted to mislead the public by distorting the Supreme Court judgment in the case of *Shayara Bano v. Union of India* (2017).[2] In the 'statement of objects and reasons' attached to the bill, the then Union Law Minister Ravi Shankar Prasad said that in spite of the Supreme Court setting aside the practice of *talaq-e-biddat* in *Shayara Bano*, there have been reports of divorce by way of such means. He described the move as an instance of 'state action to give effect to the order of the Supreme Court and to redress the grievances of victims of illegal divorce'. He also lamented that the Supreme Court verdict 'has not worked as any deterrent in bringing down the number of divorces by this practice among certain Muslims'.

DISPROPORTIONATE PUNISHMENT

The statute is a classic case of an unfair and deceptive legislative move with a populist agenda. We shall now get into the details of the mischiefs of this law, which were briefly indicated in the previous chapter. First of all, in the emblematic judgment in *Shayara Bano*, the majority on the bench had

---

[1] Martin R. Gardner, 'Illicit Legislative Motivation as a Sufficient Condition for Unconstitutionality under the Establishment Clause – A Case for Consideration: The Utah Firing Squad', *Washington University Law Review*, issue 2, 1979.

[2] On *Shayara Bano v. Union of India* (2017), see chapter 1, footnote 3.

invalidated the practice by terming it as unconstitutional. The simple and plain effect of the verdict is that the pronouncement of triple talaq by the husband is a nullity having no legal effect at all on a subsisting marriage, and despite the husband's gesture the matrimonial bond would remain intact, without being dissolved, in the eye of the law. Therefore, the enactment criminalizes an act which is *non est* in the eye of the law. The disproportionate punishment of imprisonment for three years for a civil wrong without even a civil consequence due to the Supreme Court's judgment is antithetical to the very idea of principled criminalization. Paradoxically, it was in 2018, when the bill that preceded the enactment was originally crafted, that the top court had ostensibly developed this concept by way of the verdicts on homosexuality (*Navtej Singh Johar v. Union of India* [2018])[3] and adultery (*Joseph Shine v. Union of India* [2018]).[4]

Second, the majority verdict in *Shayara Bano* did not direct the government or the Parliament to criminalize triple talaq or 'to give effect to the order', as now laid down in the Act. There was no need to do so either, as the judgment got effectuated on its own. The judgment had no intention to create any deterrent, since the very act of triple talaq is void *ab initio*, according to the Supreme Court. The Act has thus distorted the intent and content of what the court said in *Shayara Bano*. An analogy between criminalization of dowry and triple talaq does not make sense. In the case of dowry transaction is a reality, whereas in triple talaq, after the top court holding that it is a nullity, there is no act at all in the legal sense to constitute an offence. The Act thus assumes validity for an action that the court has invalidated, and as such the very thematic premise for the Act is artificial and erroneous. The settled legal principle in India that no ill motive can be attributed to legislation requires a revisit when politics overweighs constitutionalism. Third, criminalization of triple talaq can only motivate a 'skilful' husband to resort to other methods of divorce which do not fall within the ambit of the Act or to simply desert his wife. Thus, the Act does not serve Muslim women's interest.

By trying to segregate a mode of divorce in a particular community and punish men of that community alone, the centre has shattered two fundamental tenets of the Indian Constitution – equality in the eye of the law and secularism.

The Hindu, 4 January 2019, https://www.thehindu.com/opinion/op-ed/a-case-of-unprincipled-criminalisation/article25902926.ece.

---

[3] (2018) 10 SCC 1.
[4] (2019) 3 SCC 39.

3. Farm Laws, the Court and the Constitution

The agitations against the farm laws (now repealed), that started on 9 August 2020 were formally recalled on 11 December 2021. The success of the farmers' agitation against the contentious laws is a matter of solace for those who believe in the Indian constitutional ethos. This article, written during their intense struggle, tries to assess the intrinsic value of such movements, which could be relevant for the times to come.

THE CHIEF JUSTICE-LED bench of the Supreme Court observed, on 18 January 2021, that its intervention in the issue related to the new farm laws[1] has been 'misunderstood'.[2] The court's order staying the farm laws and constituting a committee has been criticized on legal and constitutional grounds. Critics say that the constitutional court tried to act as an executive court, meaning thereby that the court attempted a resolution of the issue so as to rescue the government.

The farm laws were challenged in the Supreme Court mainly on the ground that the 'pith and substance' of the legislations falls within the State List under the Seventh Schedule of the Constitution.[3] The Seventh Schedule is like a montage. For legislative purposes, often the centre intrudes into the states' terrain. A justification would then follow based on some entries in the Union List or in the Concurrent List. A whole statute will then be created resembling a script with the centre's political and economic policy. The states too sometimes might commit the same mischief. In either case, the threat to the scheme of the Constitution is writ large.

The pith and substance of the new farm laws is 'agriculture'. Agriculture,

---

[1] The Farmers' Produce Trade and Commerce (Promotion and Facilitation) Act; The Farmers' (Empowerment and Protection) Agreement of Price Assurance and Farm Services Act; and The Essential Commodities (Amendment) Act.

[2] 'Farmers' Protest: SC Refuses to Step in on Republic Day Tractor Rally', *The Hindustan Times*, 19 January 2021, https://www.hindustantimes.com/india-news/farmers-protest-sc-refuses-to-step-in-on-r-day-tractor-rally-101611001634211.html, accessed 10 December 2021.

[3] The Seventh Schedule contains the Union List, the State List and the Concurrent List. These lists indicate the respective fields over which the Parliament, or the state legislature, or both may exercise legislative power. The schedule comes under Article 246 of the Constitution which talks about 'Subject matter of laws made by Parliament and by the Legislatures of States'.

agricultural land and markets are entries 14, 18 and 28, respectively, in the State List. Entry 30 of the State List includes 'relief of agricultural indebtedness'. Entries 45 to 48 of the same list are regarding revenue and taxation related to land or agricultural land. The Supreme Court can strike down a parliamentary law if it substantially breaches the borders within the Seventh Schedule.

The judgment in *State of Bihar v. Maharajadhiraja Sir Kameshwar Singh of Darbhanga* (1952)[4] is a rare admonition against colourable legislation. In *State of Rajasthan v. G. Chawla* (1958),[5] the court focused on the content of the statute for deciding its validity. These judgments can have precedential value while scanning the farm laws. The centre would try to rely on Entry 33 in the Concurrent List. It is not a forbidden zone for the Parliament. It is an entry about trade and commerce, and also includes food items. The centre would thus try to justify its legislative competence on farm laws.

It was this constitutional conundrum that the Supreme Court was called upon to solve in the batch of cases. It could not adjudicate the issue in time and thus it contributed to the happenings in the street, though its role might have been secondary. The lesson: Time is the essence of constitutional adjudication. The court, on 12 January 2021, stayed the laws without any legal reasoning, and with clear intention to resolve the political puzzle rather than the legal puzzle. The intervention was belated and derailed. The court's committee jurisprudence has taken a good deal of flak. It was also criticized for its functional failure.

But the egregious insensitivity shown by the executive as well as the legislature is equally serious. It needed almost the whole winter in north India for the centre to suggest something significant, like keeping the laws in abeyance, to find a viable solution to the crisis. In a deliberative democracy, legislative discourse matters. Majoritarianism is not an alibi for refusing conciliation. A regime that believes in the supremacy of the market could lose sight of agonies and worries on the ground. The opposition too cannot boast of a fine track record on farmers' issues.

The farm laws were passed in Parliament with little or no deliberation in spite of protests. Deliberative democracy requires discussion and engagement

---

[4] In this case (AIR 1952 SC 252), a constitution bench of the Supreme Court considered the challenge against three state enactments – The Bihar Land Reforms Act, 1950; The Madhya Pradesh Abolition of Proprietary Rights (Estates, Mahals, Alienated Lands) Act, 1950; and The Uttar Pradesh Zamindari Abolition and Land Reforms Act, 1950. Colourable legislation happens when the legislature enacts a law on a topic by wrongly and deceptively assuming competence which it does not have.

[5] (1959) Supp (1) SCC 904.

throughout the process of law-making – before, during and after. The farmers' complaint that there was no consultation before initiating the laws shows the significance of prior deliberation. The stakeholders must be given an opportunity to be heard before significant decisions are taken that impact their interests. Natural justice is a sound principle even in the realm of law-making.

In a democracy, legitimacy of legislation is tested on the streets by peaceful agitations. Political movements are an important tool for ensuring democratic accountability. Despite the challenges posed by the pandemic, the fact that a civil agitation could be launched with enormous participation is remarkable. In general, these agitations have the potential to keep governmental actions in check. India's Civil Disobedience Movement (1930) was historic not only due to its massive character, but also on account of its roots in the ideology of non-violence. The farmers' struggle has great ethical content which is not alien to constitutionalism. This moral content is what gives strength to the movement.

Farmers have every right to seek 'justice – social, economic and political', as offered by the preamble to the country's fundamental law. Minimum support price (MSP) with statutory backing is an indispensable variation of agricultural justice. Loss of revenue for states like Punjab and Haryana due to the abolition of the *mandi* system[6] could also be a federalist concern.

The country's agricultural diversity is reflected in multiple ways and the scheme of the Seventh Schedule recognized it abundantly. Anything that weakens the federalist tenets could turn authoritarian, both in a political and an economic sense. Federalism has intrinsic democratic value.

Postscript: While updating this piece, one came across the victory march by farmers at the Singhu and Tikri protest sites, as the protest was officially called off on 11 December 2021. When the country's Constitution faced immense threat, it was not those in power but rather those who were tortured by power that tried to preserve our hard-earned freedom. This will remain a significant scripture for generations to come.

The *New Indian Express*, 24 January 2021, https://www.newindianexpress.com/opinions/2021/jan/24/farm-laws-the-court-and-the-constitution-2254192.html.

---

[6] *Mandi*s are markets created by the Agricultural Produce Market Committees (APMCs) to provide reasonable prices for agricultural produce to farmers by avoiding intermediaries, especially moneylenders. Different states have different *mandi* systems, and the governments or boards constituted by them have control over these markets.

4. Deconstructing a Draconian Law

The detention of student activists Asif Iqbal Tanha, Natasha Narwal and Devangana Kalita was based on an allegation that they instigated the local people, especially women, to agitate against the Citizenship Amendment Act, 2019. The prosecution, in quite an unconvincing way, sought to connect their protests with riots that occurred in certain parts of Delhi. The incident exposed the regime's enthusiasm to label even political criticism as a serious crime. The constitutional courts have a role to play in such contingencies. The verdict of the Delhi High Court, though belated, came as a mild solace.

'BAIL IS A constitutional recognition of the presumption of innocence', said Justice Siddharth Mridul at a CAN Foundation webinar, while addressing the issue of personal liberty in India.[1] It was the Delhi High Court bench consisting of Justices Mridul and Jairam Bhambhani that delivered the landmark verdict on 15 June 2021, by which student leaders Asif Iqbal Tanha, Natasha Narwal and Devangana Kalita were directed to be released on bail. Constitutionally guaranteed freedom is an imperative. This is a cardinal principle underlying the working of any democracy. Every judge in the country at all levels, from the trial court to the top court, is supposed to adhere to this postulate. The Delhi High Court did what it was bound to do.

But freedom is no longer taken for granted. The joy at the release of the students must not distract us from the truth of the situation where we have accepted that state-induced suffering is the order of the day. Calls for liberty, however, have been taken sometimes as judicial romanticism, given the draconian nature of certain enactments and provisions. The Unlawful Activities (Prevention) Act (UAPA), 1967, as amended from time to time, does not hold any kind of presumption of innocence. On the other hand, it poses a presumption of guilt. Therefore, Section 43(D)(5) of the Act, *inter alia,* says a person accused under the Act 'shall not be released on bail or on his own bond if the court . . . is of the opinion that there are reasonable grounds for believing that the accusation against such person is *prima facie* true'. The

---

[1] 'Bail is a Constitutional Recognition of Presumption of Innocence: Justice Siddharth Mridul at CAN Foundation Webinar', *Bar and Bench*, 21 January 2021, https://www.barandbench.com/news/litigation/bail-constitutional-recognition-presumption-of-innocence-justice-siddharth-mridul, accessed 24 December 2021.

Delhi High Court has deconstructed the harsh law, since it is convenient for any authoritarian state to level accusations against its political opponents as part of a witch-hunt. A significant character of the Narendra Modi-2 regime since 2019 is that it attacks intellectuals and activists who are not part of the established opposition, to create an atmosphere of fear. It haunts youngsters like Disha Ravi[2] or Amulya Leona Noronha[3] and elders like Stan Swamy,[4] invoking the provisions of either the Indian Penal Code (IPC) or special laws such as the UAPA. In an essay, Thulasi K. Raj and this author have explained how the UAPA becomes a tool of oppression for an illiberal state.[5]

The significance of the Delhi High Court verdict is that it tries to analyse the law with a great sense of pragmatism. When an enactment permits a time period of up to 180 days for filing the charge sheet (instead of 90 days as per the Code of Criminal Procedure [CrPC]) and allows detention of a person essentially on the basis of a false tag of terrorism, it is a crucial process that the bail court is bound to undertake. It needs to analyse the allegations in the charge sheet and see if they make out the offences as defined under the law. Solicitor General Tushar Mehta argued before the Supreme Court that the High Court had 'turned the UAPA on its head'.

The Delhi High Court has examined the charge sheet to see whether there is a *prima facie* case built under Sections 15, 17 and 18 of the UAPA, which

---

[2] Disha Ravi was accused of sharing an online document referring to the farmers' agitation, which, according to the Delhi Police, contained an 'action plan' for violence in Delhi in January 2021. Devjyot Ghoshal, 'Explainer: Why Indian Police Arrested Disha Ravi, a 22-yr-old Climate Activist', *Mint*, 16 February 2021, https://www.livemint.com/news/india/explainer-why-indian-police-arrested-disha-ravi-a-22-yr-old-climate-activist-11613468790546.html, accessed 24 December 2021.

[3] Amulya Leona Noronha, a 19-year-old student, was arrested on 20 February 2020 for shouting certain slogans which were allegedly seditious and offensive. K.M. Rakesh, 'What Sort of a Country Gangs Up on a Teen on the Basis of Half-heard Slogan?', *The Telegraph Online*, 21 February 2020, https://www.telegraphindia.com/india/what-sort-of-a-country-gangs-up-on-a-teen-on-the-basis-of-half-heard-slogan/cid/1747520 accessed 24 December 2021.

[4] Stan Swamy, a Jesuit priest and tribal rights activist, was arrested and imprisoned on the allegation that he was an activist of the Communist Party of India (Maoist), a banned organization. He died on 5 July 2021 while in judicial custody, in a private hospital. 'Explained: Who was Stan Swamy, Arrested in the Elgar Parishad Case, Who Died on July 5?', *The Indian Express*, 13 July 2021, https://indianexpress.com/article/explained/who-was-stan-swamy-6717126/, accessed 24 December 2021.

[5] Kaleeswaram Raj and Thulasi K. Raj, 'Crushing Free Spirit', *Frontline*, 19 April 2021.

talk about the offences, to satisfy the requirement of Section 43D (5) of the UAPA. Section 15 defines a terrorist act, Section 17 is about punishment for raising funds for a terrorist act, Section 18 is about punishment for conspiracy, and so on. According to Section 43D (5), before granting bail, the court should satisfy itself whether the accusation is *prima facie* true or not. When the statute demands the court to do this exercise, the state cannot find fault with the court for doing so for the sole reason that the outcome of that exercise is not in favour of the state. If the law has an inherent tendency to persuade the judge to do an act resembling a miniature trial even while considering the question of bail, it is no longer an issue with the court but with the very law. Therefore, the lamentation of the Solicitor General that the Delhi High Court practically pronounced an order of acquittal is an argument against the law itself rather than the orders of the Delhi High Court. If the High Court chose to grant bail by way of a cryptic order, the centre would have alleged non-compliance with Section 43 D (5) in the Supreme Court.

Police Behaviour

The Delhi episode is a classic case that exposes the way in which the regime stifles dissidents. Justice Madan B. Lokur, former judge of the Supreme Court, has openly criticized the Delhi Police for the way in which they dealt with the three students.[6] Whenever they were about to get bail, the police would book them for some other offence. Thereafter, the police explicitly misused the provision – that is, the proviso of Section 43D (2) in the UAPA – and often breached the limited right of the accused to get a copy of the charge sheet and to understand the allegations against them. It was on 17 September 2020 that the trial judge directed the Delhi Police to hand over the copy of the charge sheet. Instead of a hard copy of the charge sheet the students were given a copy on pen drives, which they were unable to open and read as they were in jail. The prosecution said the charge sheets ran into thousands of pages, and therefore it was expensive to get physical copies that could be given to the accused. The Delhi Police justified the delay by saying that the government would have to sanction funds to meet the expenditure to make photocopies. It was in this context that Justice Lokur wondered whether there were no financial hurdles to meeting the train and air fares to travel to Bengaluru to

[6] R. Balaji, 'Delhi Riots: Justice Lokur Castigates Cops for Mishandling of Activists', *The Telegraph Online*, 24 June 2021.

arrest the climate activist Disha Ravi (and move her to Delhi subsequently).[7]

The division bench of the Delhi High Court had examined the entire background of the case. It said in one of the orders that 'mere use of alarming and hyperbolic verbiage' in the charge sheet could not make out offences under the UAPA:

> Allegations relating to inflammatory speeches, organizing of chakka jaam, instigating women to protest and to stockpile various articles and other similar allegations, in our view, at worst, are evidence that the appellant participated in organizing protests, but we can discern no specific or particularized allegation, much less any material to bear out the allegation, that the appellant incited violence, what to talk of committing a terrorist act or a conspiracy or act preparatory to the commission of a terrorist act as understood in the UAPA.

More importantly, the court warned against 'fostering extremely grave and serious penal provisions' on citizens, observing that such a course would 'only trivialize' the provisions.

It is true that after the Supreme Court's order of 18 June 2021,[8] the Delhi High Court verdict loses precedential impact, at least for the time being. This, however, does not take away the message that it carries. When there are embargos or legal limits on granting bail or anticipatory bail under a particular enactment, it is an imperative for the court to see if the allegations make out any offence under the provisions. If they do not, bail may be granted.

STATUTORY CONTEXT

This legal position is well settled in different statutory contexts. For example, Section 18 of the Scheduled Caste and Scheduled Tribes (Prevention of Atrocities) Act, 1989 (the SC/ST Act) says that courts cannot grant anticipatory bail to any accused booked under this statute. The Supreme Court, taking note of this provision, warned that 'a duty is cast on the court to verify the averments in the complaint and to find out whether an offence under Section 3(1) of the SC/ST Act has been prima facie made out' (*Vilas Pandurang Pawar and others v. State of Maharashtra and Ors.* 2012).[9] The same position was reiterated in *Union of India v. State of Maharashtra* (2019),[10] where the apex court said

---

[7] Ibid.
[8] *State of NCT of Delhi v. Devangana Kalita* (2021), SLP (Crl.) 4289/2021.
[9] (2012)8 SCC 759.
[10] (2018)6 SCC 450.

that the bar created under Section 18 [of the SC/ST Act] on the grant of anticipatory bail is not attracted when there is 'misuse of provisions of the Act'.

Take another instance. The Muslim Women (Protection of Rights on Marriage) Act, 2019, a law brought by the Bharatiya Janata Party (BJP)-led government at the centre that criminalizes instant triple talaq, contains a somewhat analogous provision. Section 7 (c) of the enactment says that no person accused of offences under this Act shall be released on bail, unless the magistrate 'is satisfied that there are reasonable grounds for granting bail to such person'. A bench led by Justice D.Y. Chandrachud, interpreting the rider, said that 'this substantiative condition is only a recognition of something which is implicit in the judicial power to grant bail'. The court added: 'The substantive condition in Clause (c) [of Section 7] does not deprive the court of its power to grant bail.' The court emphasized that the Section did not postulate inapplicability of Section 438 of the CrPc, which grants the competent court the power to grant anticipatory bail (*Rahna Jalal vs State of Kerala*, 2020).[11]

It is not to suggest that the restriction on granting bail in these enactments are in the same manner. In the SC/ST Act it is stricter, as compared to the penal legislation on triple talaq. This has been noted in *Rahna Jalal*.[12] The irresistible conclusion is that the bail court should exercise its discretion fairly, objectively and judiciously even when the accused are booked under a stringent statute such as the UAPA. This is what the Delhi High Court has done with an elaborate judgment. These decisions of the apex court also show the way out for a country that is suppressed by an aggrandizing executive that constantly invokes 'the terror of laws'.[13]

However, despite these judgments, the top court was unable to act in many instances where it was supposed to act. This led to the continued incarceration of many, including the accused in the Bhima Koregaon case. An exception, however, was the stay order against the coercive steps against two Telugu channels.[14] It said that certain sections in the IPC – Section 124A (sedition),

---

[11] (2021) 1 SCC 733.

[12] Ibid.

[13] Venkitesh Ramakrishnan and Divya Trivedi, 'The Terror of Laws', *Frontline*, 9 April 2021.

[14] The allegation against the two channels, TV5 and ABN, was that they telecast programmes critical of the Government of Andhra Pradesh and the state's Chief Minister. An FIR was registered under various sections of the IPC. It was a 'suo moto case' registered as per an enquiry report prepared by a police officer. Order dated 31 May 2021 in *M/S Aamoda Broadcasting Company Private Limited and Anr v. The State of Andhra Pradesh and Ors.* (2021), WP(Crl.) 217/2021.

Section 153A (promoting enmity in society) and Section 505 (statements conducing to public mischief) – would need a revisit 'particularly in the context of the right of the electronic and print media to communicate news, information and the rights, even those that may be critical of the prevailing regime in any part of the nation'.[15]

The Delhi High Court verdict has great educative value for institutions. The top court is considering the challenge against certain amendments made to the UAPA in 2019.[16] The court has already admitted challenges against the sedition law under Section 124A of the IPC, an equally misused provision (*Kishorechandra Wangkhemcha and Anr. v. Union of India*, order dated 30 April 2021).[17] The Supreme Court has interpreted the provisions in UAPA in a relatively liberal way in a later case, which we shall discuss in chapter 24. Sooner or later, the apex court may have to strike down these draconian enactments for ostensible reasons. But until then, the courts in India dealing with citizen's liberty must act prudently, fairly and democratically. Viewed in this way, every court, including the trial court, is performing the duties of safeguarding constitutional rights. The legal and political fraternity need to re-educate the judicial institutions and the individuals running them.

Frontline, 16 July 2021, https://frontline.thehindu.com/cover-story/deconstructing-a-draconian-law-uapa-delhi-high-court-verdict-granting-bail-to-student-activists-natasha-narwal-devangana-kalita-asif-iqbal-tanha/article35053191.ece.

---

[15] Order referred in footnote 12 above.
[16] Nilashish Chaudhary, 'SC Issues Notice on Plea Challenging Validity of UAPA Amendment', *Live Law*, 6 September 2019, https://www.livelaw.in/top-stories/sc-issues-notice-on-plea-challenging-validity-of-uapa-amendment-147821, accessed 24 December 2021.
[17] (2021) 6 SCC 177.

PART TWO

ON THE COURTS

5. The Pressing Need to Adjudicate, Not Mediate

In chapter 3, Part One, we noted the content of the farm laws. Here, the focus is on the role of the courts in such matters. When political issues are fought in courts, the country may witness mass movements and a national discourse on the process of adjudication. This article was written in the context of a court order on protests against the amendments in the citizenship law and the agitations against 'the farm laws'. The farm laws have now been repealed, but criticism of the court's approach remains relevant and valid.

THE JUDGMENT OF the Supreme Court on 7 October 2020 that refused to review its earlier verdict on the Shaheen Bagh protest[1] is inseparable from its political context. The verdict declared that there is no absolute right to protest, and it could be subjected to the orders of the authority regarding place and time. Apart from thinking about the legal and constitutional issues, it can also lead to a discourse on the moral authority of the top court in dealing with such fundamental questions related to freedom.

PROTESTS: A POLITICAL CHALLENGE

Both the judgments came out at the time of ongoing street agitations. Protest 'at any time and everywhere'[2] has not been as simple as conceived

---

[1] The non-violent protest opposing the Citizenship (Amendment) Act started on 15 December 2019 and continued till March 2020. The agitators at the site, Shaheen Bagh, predominantly included Muslim women. Many Muslims in India were unhappy with the criteria stipulated for grant of citizenship to migrants from the neighbouring countries. Muslims from those countries were not to be given citizenship even if they were persecuted there. More than this, the grievance of the Muslim minority in India was about the proposed National Citizenship Register (NRC). This might require people belonging to minority communities to prove their citizenship with ancestorial documents – a task that is difficult and often impossible. The protesters were anxious about recognition of their political identity as citizens rather than their religious identity. Still, the Shaheen Bagh protest was criticized by sections of the population alleging that it caused blockade of roads and inconvenience to the 'public'.

[2] *Kaniz Fatima and Ors. v. Commissioner of Police and Ors.*, 9 February 2021, Review Petition (Civil) Diary No. 24552/2020 in Civil Appeal No. 3282/2020.

in the judgments. The agitations against the Citizenship (Amendment) Act (CAA)[3] and the farm laws[4] also brought out the immense agony and hardship that the protesters had to face. In the anti-farm laws struggle, they experienced suffering over almost the entire winter for a cause they believed to be one that concerns the whole nation. They had to pay a heavy price for their conviction. Many were subjected to malicious prosecution by the state on serious charges of sedition and terrorist activities. Not only the protesters but also their supporters, including comedians, journalists and other media persons, were charged. All freedoms under Article 19 of the Constitution, from freedom of expression to that of peaceful association, were seriously impaired.

Even today, many languish in jail for the offence of dissent and the more serious offence of '*andolan*'. Disha Ravi, a 22-year-old climate activist, was booked in February 2021 for 'conspiracy against the government'. Such arrests continue because the protests are a political challenge to the existing regime, a theme which the court did not even address with contextual details.

A PROBLEMATIC 'BALANCING'

There is a more significant question that a citizen could pose against the court's pronouncements on the Shaheen Bagh protest. Agitation on the street became an imperative because the issues were not subjected to a timely judicial examination. The subject matter of almost all the major protests that have happened recently in India, be it over 'economic reservation', the CAA or the farm laws, involved legal and constitutional issues requiring immediate and effective adjudication in terms of their constitutional validity. The top court could not exercise its constitutional role and ensure judicial scrutiny over an aggrandizing executive and an equally imposing Parliament by carrying out its counter-majoritarian function. Having failed to do so, the kind of 'balancing' the court tried to attain by way of the Shaheen Bagh orders will pose more questions than it answers.

---

[3] See chapters 1, 26 and 28.

[4] The three contentious farm laws were The Farmers' Produce Trade and Commerce (Promotion and Facilitation) Act 2020, The Farmers (Empowerment and Protection) Agreement on Price Assurance and Farm Services Act, and the Essential Commodities (Amendment) Act 2020. As a result of the historic agitation by the farmers' associations, the laws were taken back by the centre. However, the need to have timely determination of constitutional issues warrants further deliberations.

In the original judgment on Shaheen Bagh,[5] the court attempted to 'mediate' the issue and admitted that it 'did not produce any solution'. The court's duty during testing times is to adjudicate, not to mediate. A reconciliatory approach is not a substitute for juridical assertion. The review petition provided the Supreme Court an opportunity to revisit its earlier folly where it merely acted as a judicial extension of the executive. It could have taken empirical lessons from a political situation that was, at certain levels, almost proximate to an internal emergency.

Constitutional morality is a philosophy that should primarily apply to the constitutional courts. Dr B.R. Ambedkar used this idea in terms of institutions and not merely in terms of individuals. Had there been a timely adjudication of the validity of the laws which was questioned by the process recognized by the law, the torment on the street probably could have been reduced.

THINK FAIR AND EFFECTIVE

A fair and effective adjudicative mechanism in constitutional matters can meaningfully sublimate the agitation on the street. Studies have shown that social movements could be less radical and less oppositional when issues are effectively sorted out by way of fair litigative means. The sociologist Luke Martell said that the radical green movement in Britain moved at a slower pace when compared with other parts of Western Europe, because the 'public enquiry system' in the United Kingdom could 'process ecological demands, integrate them into the political system and minimize radicalization of the movement arising out of exclusion and marginalization'.[6] This principle can have application across constitutional democracies.

The textbook theory of 'balancing' the right to protest and the right to move along the road does not need any reiteration in the constitutional climate of the present day. When fear is the new normal for the average Indian, the court's only role is to act as the guardian of the right to dissent.

In the review petition,[7] the petitioners rightly apprehended that the observations in the earlier judgment against the indefinite occupation of public space 'may prove to be a licence in the hands of the police to commit atrocities on legitimate voice of protest'. The court, by its rejection of the plea, has reinforced an illiberal state's intimidating stand in another unjust

---

[5] *Amit Sahni v. Commissioner of Police*, 7 October 2020, Civil Appeal No. 3282/2020.

[6] Luke Martell, *Ecology and Society*, Cambridge: Polity Press, 1994.

[7] See Kaniz Fatima's case noted above.

political situation. Its affirmation of the earlier view is not merely insensitive or surreal; it illustrates an instance of 'abusive judicial review', as described by Landau and Dixon,[8] where the court not only refuses to act as the umpire of democracy but aids the executive in fulfilling its strategies. In the process, it legitimizes very many illegitimate state actions.

STATE'S INTRUSION IS A WORRY

In the 2020 verdict, the Supreme Court has also failed to properly appreciate and contextualize the earlier constitution bench judgment in *Himat Lal K. Shah v. Commissioner of Police* (1972),[9] even after referring to it. It is the state's intrusion into the realm of rights that should worry the court. In *Himat Lal K. Shah*, the court said that the rule framed by the Ahmedabad Police Commissioner conferred arbitrary power on the police officers in the matter of public meetings, and therefore was liable to be struck down. Justice Kuttyil Kurien Mathew, in this case, explained that 'freedom of assembly is an essential element of a democratic system' and that 'the public streets are the "natural" places for expression of opinion and dissemination of ideas'.

In the review petition, it was not the cause alone that was tried. It was also the court.

The Hindu, 19 February 2021, https://www.thehindu.com/opinion/lead/the-pressing-need-to-adjudicate-not-mediate/article33874422.ece.

[8] David Landau and Rosalind Dixon, 'Abusive Judicial Review: Courts against Democracy', *Davis Law Review*, vol. 53, University of California, 2020, pp. 1313–87.
[9] (1973) 1 SCC 227. In connection with a national students' strike sponsored by the All India Students Federation (AISF), a petition was moved before the public commissioner for permission to hold a public meeting, which was refused. This was the subject of the legal challenge.

6. A New Jurisprudence

In the chapters in Part One of this volume, an attempt has been made to analyse the stringent nature of certain recent laws, many of which impact the liberty of the citizen in a drastic way. This article poses the need for developing a new jurisprudence to counter the narrative of the political executive. This is a task that the Supreme Court must take up.

THE OBSERVATIONS OF Justice D.Y. Chandrachud while considering the bail application of Arnab Goswami[1] reflected the spirit of the Constitution. The judge said that if the top court does not interfere in the event of an illegal arrest, 'we are travelling a path of destruction'. Liberty of the individual is the first promise of the fundamental law. While the procedural prescriptions in the Code of Criminal Procedure (CrPC) that mandate the filing of bail applications before the competent court need to be the norm, those should not prevent the top court from invoking its jurisdiction to favour liberty in critical situations. Justice Chandrachud's dissenting view in the Bhima Koregaon case (*Romila Thapar and Ors. v. Union of India and Ors.* [2018]),[2] in which he advocated for liberty of the activists and their right to a fair investigation, was more than a dissent. Judicial history demonstrates that dissents from the bench during unjust political situations have acted as

---

[1] The allegation against Goswami was that he owed a huge amount of money to Anvay Naik, an architect, who designed the television studio for Goswami. Naik committed suicide in 2018. His wife alleged that Goswami, who did not pay her husband the fee due to him, was responsible for the suicide. According to Goswami, the very allegation was false, and foisted, and the Government of Maharashtra was taking a vindicative measure against him due to political animosity.

[2] The judgment in this case filed by *Romila Thapar and Ors.* (2018) 10 SCC 753 deals with the plea for release of five prominent persons, namely Gautam Navlakha, Sudha Bharadwaj, Varavara Rao, Arun Ferreira and Vernon Gonsalves. They were arrested on 28 August 2018. The arrest was allegedly 'without any credible material and evidence'. The allegation was that they had 'caused incitement and violence at Bhima Koregaon on 1 January 2018'. There was allegation about their 'involvement in planning the assassination of the current prime minister'. Also, there were allegations of Maoist links. But later on, a US-based digital forensic firm, Arsenal Consulting, claimed that incriminating letters in the case were actually planted in the computer recovered from the house of Rona Wilson, yet another accused arrested in connection with the Bhima Koregaon case.

long-term institutional critique, persuading the court to introspect. As Justice Charles Evans Hughes has described, those were intended for 'the intelligence of the future day'.[3]

Viewed so, the criticism of the court by the comedian Kunal Kamra,[4] again, is an institutional criticism in a different language. The tweets may be annoying or shocking to a conventional mindset. The fact that the attorney general granted sanction to prosecute Kamra does not mean that he is guilty. It does not even mean that the court will initiate action for contempt. Rule 3 of the rules to regulate proceedings for contempt of the Supreme Court, 1975, says that the attorney general's consent is needed to examine a petition seeking initiation of contempt proceedings. It only means that the top court gets an opportunity to go deeper into the content of the criticism while deciding whether the comedian should be proceeded against.

The entire criticism of the Supreme Court has a constitutional basis, as Article 14 of the Indian Constitution promises equality before the law and equal protection of the laws. *Al Jazeera* reported that 'India's Supreme Court [is] in [the] spotlight over bail for divisive anchor'.[5] In a report in *The Wire*,[6] Ismat Ara and Sukanya Shantha have given a long list of activists, journalists and politicians who are incarcerated in different jails in the country as their bail applications were rejected.

How the Supreme Court has attempted to change its philosophy on rights and its public image immediately after the Emergency is a crucial lesson in India's legal history. What one should be careful to find out is the invisible linkage between the dissent, say, of Justice H.R. Khanna,[7] and the

---

[3] As cited in *K.S. Puttaswamy and Anr. v Union of India* (2017) 10 SCC 1, para 447.

[4] Kamra criticized the Supreme Court in a series of tweets for granting interim bail to Arnab Goswami. He implied that the Supreme Court failed to safeguard the liberty of other citizens, including journalists, activists and intellectuals, while granting relief to Goswami.

[5] Valay Singh, 'India's Supreme Court in Spotlight Over Bail for Divisive Anchor', *Al Jazeera*, 13 November 2020, https://www.aljazeera.com/news/2020/11/13/india-top-court-under-fire-for-bailing-out-divisive-tv-presenter, accessed 14 December 2021.

[6] Ismat Ara and Sukanya Santha, 'A List of Activists, Scholars and Scribes Whose Personal Liberty Remains at Judiciary's Mercy', *The Wire*, 13 November 2020, https://thewire.in/rights/jail-bail-hearings-court-delhi-riots-elgar-parishad, accessed 14 December 2021.

[7] In *ADM Jabalpur v. Shivkant Shukla* (1976) 2 SCC 521, while the majority of the judges took the view that the fundamental rights could be suspended on proclamation of Emergency, Justice Khanna alone dissented and held that even

perceptions of the later Supreme Court. The Supreme Court is criticized for the alleged selective approach, rather than for granting bail to the television journalist. One could think that in a given case, the court is concerned only with legal adjudication rather than an ethical or political assessment of the individual or the causes that led to the individual's predicament. The legal constitutionalism adopted by the Chandrachud–Banerjee bench, however, cannot erase the relevance of the criticism of the court as an institution, which is essentially based on political constitutionalism.

The legal scholar Marco Goldoni, while dealing with the limits and possibilities of political constitutionalism, has described its tenets and said that political equality is its 'reference point'. He says that 'while equality before the law (isonomia) is certainly to be counted among the founding principles of legal constitutionalism, political equality as the equal chance to have one's voice heard (isegoria) constitutes the building block of democratic politics'.[8]

It follows, therefore, that political criticism of the court as an institution belongs to a broader realm and has deeper connotations. Such criticisms of the court have arisen in very many constitutional democracies and dictatorial democracies in recent times. These are not directed against the attitude of the courts alone; they are also about the legislative gestures that enacted the draconian laws and the executive postures that invoked them. As such, Kamra's criticism needs to be analysed in the light of the factors that encourage the present day's aggrandizing executive, a legislature that made it and a judiciary impacted by it. On closer scrutiny, even the offensive vocabulary in Kamra's tweets would call for such deeper analysis.

The state has been misusing the Unlawful Activities (Prevention) Act along with the penal provisions on sedition quite selectively. Equally rampant has been the misuse of Section 144 of the CrPC to suppress peaceful protests. The riots in Delhi exposed a partisan police with scant regard for the rule of law or the sense of justice. Frequent preventive arrests reminded one of the days of the Emergency (1975–77). In several cases, dissidents were booked and kept in jail. The state rigorously opposed their bail applications, and the trial courts or the high courts, as the case may be, very often declined bail.

---

during Emergency 'the state has got no power to deprive a person of his life or personal liberty without the authority of law'.

[8] Marco Goldoni, 'Two Internal Critiques of Political Constitutionalism', *International Journal of Constitutional Law*, vol. 10, no. 4, October 2012, pp. 926–49, https://doi.org/10.1093/icon/mos033.

The 'apathy' of the high court in these cases is more or less similar to the situation in Goswami's case that annoyed the highest court.

The top court has to take stock of these episodes, consider them as a batch of cases involving individual liberty under Articles 19 (freedom of speech and expression) and 21 (protection of life and personal liberty) of the Constitution, and immediately set the detainees free after imposing conditions if required. These cases may differ in terms of facts, but there could be more similarities and common factors among all of them which, if not addressed immediately, could take us to 'the path of destruction'. This, the Supreme Court can do even by invoking Article 142 of the Constitution, which is meant to do 'complete justice'. The scope of Article 142 in the context of liberty was explained by Justice Chandrachud in the case of Romila Thapar's dissent. It may be difficult for one to imagine such a legal scenario, but it is not impossible legally or constitutionally.

We need to develop a new jurisprudence on institutional criticism, especially that concerning the courts. The existence of the law of criminal contempt and laws on sedition will have to be dealt with in that adjudicative exercise. It is not the misuse of these laws but their very existence that threatens our democracy. An approach will have to be evolved that limits the use of such laws to only those cases that pose real and immanent threat to the nation. Perhaps, the Kunal Kamra episode poses fundamental questions relating to our democracy which the Supreme Court may have to address by invoking its introspective jurisdiction, even by taking a clue from what Justice Chandrachud said while considering the plea by Goswami.

The Telegraph, 1 December 2020, https://www.telegraphindia.com/opinion/the-laws-on-contempt-and-sedition-threaten-democracy/cid/1799077.

7. On the Apex Court's Moral Authority

Isolated incidents in the court can ignite discourse on the ethics of the individuals and institutions. This article was written in the context of Justice Arun Mishra refusing to recuse from hearing a batch of land acquisition cases. After his retirement, Justice Mishra was appointed chairman of the National Human Rights Commission (NHRC).

'WE MAY TRY to see things as objectively as we please. Nonetheless, we can never see them with any eyes except our own', said Benjamin Cardozo, former American Supreme Court judge.[1] Any adjudicative process could invariably involve an inescapable element of subjectivity. Still, conceptually, an impartial and unbiased court is a constitutional promise and as such a citizen's right. So, the point is to mitigate not only bias but also the appearance of bias in the decision-making process. This is a well-accepted legal principle.

On 23 October 2019, a constitution bench of the Supreme Court rejected the plea for the recusal of Justice Arun Mishra from the bench considering a provision in a land acquisition statute. Curiously enough, the request for the recusal of Justice Mishra was rejected by Justice Mishra himself, who headed the constitution bench and wrote the main judgment. Other judges on the bench concurred with Justice Mishra by way of a separate opinion.

Let us consider the details. A three-judge bench delivered a judgment in 2014 on Section 24 of the Right to Fair Compensation and Transparency in Land Acquisition, Rehabilitation and Resettlement Act, 2013. It interpreted the provision so as to benefit the land owners who suffered acquisition, to a considerable extent. It extended the benefit of the new Act to the land owners in certain specified contingencies, even though the acquisition was under the old colonial Act of 1894.

The verdict also benefited many. In 2018, strangely enough, after a reference, another three-judge bench led by Justice Mishra, with one judge dissenting, not only doubted the correctness of the 2014 judgment but also overruled it. This exercise was clearly wrong. It was a glaring instance of judicial indiscipline. A coordinate bench could not have overruled the law

---

[1] Benjamin N. Cardozo, *The Nature of Judicial Process*, New York: Dover Publications, 2012.

laid down by a bench of similar strength. Another bench, consisting of the judges who delivered the 2014 verdict, noted this impropriety and passed an order putting on hold the cases involving the same legal question.

The issue thus had to be referred to the constitution bench, which was headed by Justice Mishra. A demand for his recusal followed. The objectors apprehended judicial obstinacy on the part of Justice Mishra since the bench led by him had overruled the verdict by a co-equal bench. They relied on a verdict in *State of West Bengal and Ors. v. Shivananda Pathak and Ors.* (1998)[2] that explained the mischiefs of judicial obstinacy. Rejecting the objections, Justice Mishra wrote: 'Recusal is not to be forced by any litigant to choose a Bench. It is for the Judge to decide to recuse.' The first proposition is indisputable; the second one, however, is problematic.

The issue of recusal cannot be discussed in isolation. Nor can it be seen in the abstract. It needs a contextual examination. Justice Mishra's judgment relies on instances where the doubting judges in the earlier benches were part of subsequent larger benches deciding the correctness of conflicting views. Those instances were, however, clearly dissimilar. No case cited by Justice Mishra in the order involved a case of an impermissible annulment of a judgment by a co-ordinate bench. There are no precedents on facts and no judgment can ever be read like a statute.

Each case needs a decision based on its own facts and circumstances. The present imbroglio, in that sense, is unique and unprecedented; it needed an innovative solution on its own, which was quite simple and possible. The Chief Justice, who is the master of the roster, could have constituted the bench by annihilating any apprehension by looking into the episodes that led to the present perplexity. Given that there are thirty-four judges in the top court, a legal issue impacting thousands of people with an unprecedented chronology could have been resolved with a better sense of judicial statesmanship. The episode puts up a strong case for judicious internal management for the court. The issue is not just legal; it is also administrative.

Sarah Cravens indicates that a system should strive not for appearance of justice but actual justice itself, in the process of adjudication.[3] In an ideal situation, even a judge who is predisposed on a legal proposition could be persuaded to change his views. But situations are not always ideal. Judges do not always function like gods. Psychology talks about unconscious bias,

---

[2] (1998) 5 SCC 513.

[3] Sarah M.R. Cravens, 'In Pursuit of Actual Justice', *Alabama Law Review*, vol. 59, 2007.

and judges could be vulnerable to it. The 'duty to sit doctrine', evolved in the US, has formidable critics. The doctrine holds that sitting should be the rule and recusal, the exception. To minimize the demand for recusal and thereby uphold the majesty of the institution, a strategy to get ideal persons on the bench is an imperative. Almost every problem connected with the Indian judiciary has an invisible but real nexus with its outdated method of judicial selection, based on considerations that remain unknown to the people at large.

It may not be desirable to enact a parliamentary law to deal with the situation, for that would lead to a breach of conventionally accepted principles regarding the separation of powers. As indicated by legal scholar James Sample, 'The teachable moments on disqualification are in the Court's court.'[4] Former American Supreme Court judge Robert Jackson once said: 'We are not final because we are infallible, but we are infallible only because we are final.'[5] The order declining recusal is final, but it sets a bad precedent. It has legal force, but no moral authority.

The New Indian Express, 1 November 2019, https://www.newindianexpress.com/opinions/2019/nov/01/on-the-apex-courts-moral-authority-2055451.html.

---

[4] James J. Sample, 'Supreme Court Recusal: From Marbury to the Modern Day', *Georgetown Journal of Ethics*, vol. 26, 2013, p. 95.
[5] *Brown v. Allen* 344 US 443, 540 (1950).

8. Fighting Corruption in the Judiciary

This article on judicial corruption pleads for a comprehensive legislation to ensure the accountability of judges. A non-statutory code of conduct has not yielded any positive result in the Indian context.

IN 2019, FORMER Chief Justice of India Ranjan Gogoi granted permission to the Central Bureau of Investigation (CBI) to register a First Information Report (FIR) against Justice S.N. Shukla of the Allahabad High Court.[1] This unprecedented step was taken immediately after the Chief Justice's letter to Prime Minister Narendra Modi to move for impeachment of Justice Shukla. An enquiry panel constituted by the then Chief Justice of India, Dipak Misra, found that there was substance in the allegations against the judge. The main allegation was that the judge had abused his judicial authority to favour a Lucknow-based medical college to unauthorizedly admit students of the 2017–18 batch.

The enquiry panel in Shukla's case reportedly said that the judge has 'disgraced the values of judicial life, acted in a manner unbecoming of a judge to lower the majesty, dignity and credibility of his office'. Therefore, ideally, any act or omission that negates the values of judicial life should fall within the ambit of judicial corruption and one should comprehend it beyond the provisions of the Prevention of Corruption Act (1988).

Benjamin N. Cardozo has conceived judicial process as a serene one that tries to reach the goal of justice with an uncompromising adherence to objectivity of assessment. On adjudication, he has said that 'in the endless process of testing and retesting, there is a constant rejection of the dross, and a constant retention of whatever is pure and sound and fine'.[2] Legal scholar J.A.G. Griffith, in his seminal work *The Politics of the Judiciary*, quotes the English political theorist H.J. Laski who said that 'nothing is more disastrous than that any suspicion of the complete impartiality of the judges should

---

[1] Dhananjay Mahapatra, 'In a 1st, CJI Allows CBI to File Case Against HC Judge', *The Times of India*, 31 July 2019, http://timesofindia.indiatimes.com/ articleshow/70457309.cms?from=mdr&utm_source=contentofinterest&utm_ medium=text&utm_campaign=cppst, accessed 14 December 2021.
[2] Benjamin N. Cardozo, *The Nature of the Judicial Process*, Delhi: Universal Law Publish-ing Co., reprint, 2004.

be possible'.[3] Therefore, the end of faith in the judiciary can lead to serious repercussions.

Any activity or behaviour that meddles with the quality of justice should be a matter of concern. We do not have any comprehensive law addressing aberrations on and off the bench. But the code of conduct for judges evolved in the Bangalore Convention[4] is one that is internationally acknowledged. A round table meeting of Chief Justices from different jurisdictions ratified it at The Hague in November 2002. It speaks about independence, impartiality, integrity, propriety, sense of equality, competence and diligence as fundamental judicial values. It is an ethical reminder to every robed functionary in the courts and the tribunals. But there is a striking dichotomy between what is written on paper and what occurs on the ground. The infamous collegium system has developed a kind of 'homo social morphing' whereby judges select judges according to their own notions of justice and justicing, without any due process and often based on mysterious considerations.

No wonder that the country is no longer capable of routinely selecting a Krishna Iyer, P.B. Gajendragadkar or K.K. Mathew for the bench. On the other hand, we find a judge in the Rajasthan High Court declaring that peacocks do not have sex, and a Meghalaya judge requesting Prime Minister Modi to deal with the citizenship and domicile related issues, since according to him, right in 1947 itself, India 'should . . . have been declared . . . a Hindu country'. A Kerala judge also courted controversy with his casteist remarks glorifying Brahmins. None of these incidents has a connection with any kind of corruption. But these incidents speak of the quality of their understanding of justice and also of the justice that they render. One should however note that there are very many erudite judges in the country who function in an admirable way. The 'bad apples' need segregation.

A non-statutory code of conduct may not be adequate for clearing the system. A comprehensive legislation to ensure judicial accountability is an imperative. The fundamental solution lies in selecting the right people for the tough job. There has to be a formal mechanism based on equality of opportunity and transparency in the process of judicial selection, and the independent commissions in advanced democracies indicate the way ahead. Only a systemic change can make a difference.

An assertive bar and a responsible media can, from within the bounds

---

[3] J.A.G. Griffith, *The Politics of the Judiciary*, Manchester: Manchester University Press, 1977.

[4] Judicial Integrity Group on Strengthening Judicial Integrity, 2000.

of law, judge the judges and guard the guards. The legal profession has become so hierarchical that it has lost its egalitarian and critical impulses. A professional seldom wants to be a reformer and the path ahead for a reformer is quite thorny. Star lawyers create an artificial and mythical aura around them. No wonder, reformative movements are fast disappearing within the institution of the judiciary. Ordinary lawyers across the country have become a frustrated lot, and their helplessness reflects the agony of the masses who are consumers of an imperilled justice system. The oppositional radicalism of an organized bar combating judicial misbehaviour is only a form of nostalgia that the legal fraternity silently shares.

One dreams a possible utopia in Indian courts while reading Daniel Webster, who said: 'There is no happiness, there is no liberty, there is no enjoyment of life, unless a man can say when he rises in the morning, I shall be subject to the decision of no unjust judge today.'

Postscript: This article started with Justice Ranjan Gogoi's nod to proceed against a High Court judge. We shall discuss more about Justice Gogoi in the next chapter and chapter 16.

The New Indian Express, 12 August 2019, https://www.newindianexpress.com/opinions/2019/aug/12/fighting-corruption-in-judiciary-2017673.html.

9. Addressing Judicial Misbehaviour

The behaviour of judges, on and off the bench, can have far-reaching consequences in the lives of the people and for the well-being of democracy. Judicial misbehaviour is seldom addressed by those at the helm of affairs. A constitutional mechanism is needed to deal with the alleged wrongs committed by judges.

Simon Rifkind, a well-known American jurist, once said: 'The courtroom, sooner or later, becomes the image of the judge. It will rise or fall to the level of the judge who presides over it.' Therefore, the image of the judge is fundamental for the institution. In the words of American lawyer and academic Alan Dershowitz, 'judges are the weakest link in our system of justice, and they are also the most protected'.

On 20 April 2019, the Supreme Court said that the accusation against Justice Ranjan Gogoi, the then Chief Justice of India, made by a female employee of the court was 'wild and baseless, designed to attack and erode the independence of the judiciary'.[1] Chief Justice Gogoi said that there was a 'bigger plot' 'to deactivate' his office.[2] The country debated on the level of protection that the Chief Justice can have. In *K. Veeraswami v. Union of India and Ors.* (1991),[3] the Supreme Court had said that 'the judges are liable to

---

[1] Samanwaya Rautray, 'Judiciary Under Attack, Says SC Bench on Allegations against Chief Justice Ranjan Gogoi', *The Economic Times*, 20 April 2019, https://economictimes.indiatimes.com/news/politics-and-nation/judiciary-under-attack-says-sc-bench-on-allegations-against-chief-justice-ranjan-gogoi/articleshow/68963846.cms, accessed 15 December 2021.

[2] 'Chief Justice Says Sexual Harassment Charge Part of "Bigger Plot" to "Deactivate" Him', *The Wire*, 20 April 2019, https://thewire.in/law/supreme-court-special-sitting-cji-ranjan-gogoi-allegations, accessed 15 December 2021.

[3] (1991) 3 SCC 655. A complaint was filed before the Central Bureau of Investigation (CBI) against Justice Veeraswami, the then Chief Justice of Madras High Court, alleging offences under the Prevention of Corruption Act. A first information report was launched based on it and subsequently, a charge sheet was filed. The allegation was about amassing of wealth disproportionate to known sources of income. The special court issued process to the judge, who had retired by then, requiring his presence in court. The judge challenged it in the High Court, and the High Court rejected the challenge. Against the decision of the High Court, the judge then approached the Supreme Court. The Supreme Court delivered its judgment on 25 July 1991.

be dealt with just the same way as any other person in respect of criminal offence'. But the *Veeraswami* verdict also held that the consent of the Chief Justice of India (CJI) is required to register a first information report (FIR) against a judge of the High Court or the Supreme Court. If the accusation is against the CJI, permission by 'any other judge or judges of the Supreme Court' is needed.

The apex court is in deep crisis. The way in which an allegation of a serious nature was dealt with has tarnished the image of the institution.[4] A committee consisting of only judges enquired into the matter as per the in-house procedure evolved by the court. The proceedings were secret and so was the outcome. The reasons for the clean chit given to the then CJI, Ranjan Gogoi, still remain unknown.

Equality before law and equal protection of the law are constitutional imperatives as evident from Article 14. The rule of law within the judiciary is a condition precedent for the rule of law outside. A constitutional court has to set an example for constitutional morality in every facet of its functioning. It needs to evolve a credible and efficacious method to deal with critical situations that should satisfy the constitutional test and the requirements of natural justice. The in-house mechanism and the *Veeraswami* methodology are far from satisfactory in this regard.

A few lawyers, however, supported the in-house procedure as one in tune with the law on the point. Because the members of the committee are Supreme Court judges, they say, the procedures are fault-free and unquestionable. They say that secrecy is the rule and openness is not even the exception. No legal representation, no access to the findings, no questions, no criticism. They presumed that the court can act like an 'imperium in imperio', as lamented by T.T. Krishnamachari long ago during the Constituent Assembly debates. They were, no doubt, defending the indefensible.

No democracy can sustain itself by converting public offices into theatres. We need to be wise enough to learn empirical lessons on the issue from elsewhere. When Brett Kavanaugh was nominated as an associate judge of the Supreme Court of the US in 2018, allegations of sexual harassment were raised by a female professor, Christine Blasey Ford. The alleged incident,

---

[4] The case alleging sexual harassment against the then Chief Justice Ranjan Gogoi had a curious turn. A three-judge bench of the Supreme Court, of which Justice Gogoi also was part, considered the issue. Subsequently, there was an in-house probe into the matter, which also lacked transparency or procedural fairness. Read more on this in chapter 16.

according to Ford, occurred in 1982 when both of them were studying in high school. After Ford, two other women also raised allegations of sexual misconduct against Kavanaugh. A probe by independent agencies followed, the records of which are in the public domain even now. Ultimately, however, on 6 October 2018, Kavanaugh's nomination was confirmed by a thin majority in the Senate.

In an earlier episode, Anita Hill, a lawyer, publicly deposed before the US Senate Committee about alleged sexual harassment by Clarence Thomas, whose elevation as a judge of the top court in the US was pending consideration. The complaint was dismissed after an open Senate hearing.

Accusations against sitting judges have occurred in other jurisdictions as well. Sir Stephen Richards, a judge of the Court of Appeal in the UK, was arrested and prosecuted for the alleged offence of bad conduct with women while travelling in a train. In one case, he was tried by the Westminster Magistrates' Court and acquitted. In another case, prosecution was dropped. Samuel Kent, a federal court judge in the US, was accused of sexual misconduct and lying to the investigators. He was found guilty, and was sentenced on 11 May 2009 with a fine and imprisonment. He had to resign after facing impeachment.

Such incidents had the ostensible effect of enhancing the credibility of the judiciary in these countries. The episodes illustrate that judges too are governed by the laws of the nation.

The in-house procedure in India is not one made by legislation. It is a self-regulatory device adopted by the Supreme Court in 1999. There is no empirical evidence to indicate its capacity to render justice to the aggrieved. No judge in the country has ever been subjected to any serious action by such a mechanism, even though there have been at least a few accusations.

Who will judge the judges is a fundamental question of Indian democracy, and we need to address it. A constitutional mechanism to deal with judicial misbehaviour and the crimes committed by judges needs to be designed by way of a comprehensive legislation. This needs to be done without compromising judicial independence and also by adhering to the principles of equality. The law of the land does not, and cannot, create immunity for persons holding high constitutional posts.

The New Indian Express, 16 May 2019, https://www.newindianexpress.com/opinions/2019/may/16/addressing-judicial-misbehaviour-1977565.html.

10. The Supreme Court of India: In a Different Epoch

The article considers a few instances where the Supreme Court failed to interfere with some key issues concerning the whole nation. We need to recognize the quintessential relation between politics and the law.

THE SUPREME COURT has been criticized for its failure to act as the guardian of the Constitution. Issues ranging from demonetization to Kashmir, and the indiscriminate arrest and detention of intellectuals and activists, met with an inert Supreme Court. The court often deferred the adjudication or relegated it to others. On other occasions, it abruptly declined to entertain significant pleas having political and economic ramifications. On issues like the desirability of the Central Vista project[1] and the accountability attached to the PM CARES Fund,[2] it refused to pass any interdicting orders. Writ petitions challenging the dilution of labour laws were abruptly dismissed.

The aim of this article is not to repeat the criticisms against the Supreme Court. The questions it raises are as follows. What is the reason for such conduct of the court at a critical time? What are the ways to overcome this 'pathological period', to borrow the phrase of Professor Vincent Blasi?

---

[1] The project intends to restructure the country's central administrative area in New Delhi. The multi-crore construction was opposed by many concerned citizens on legal, economic, ecological and other grounds. The project reflected wrong priority during the economic and health crisis due to the Covid-19 pandemic. The Delhi High Court dismissed the plea and imposed a cost of Rs 1 lakh on the petitioner. The top court refused to entertain the appeal against this verdict. See, Krishnadas Rajagopal, 'Central Vista Project: SC Dismisses Plea Against Delhi HC Verdict Refusing to Halt Work', *The Hindu*, 29 June 2021, https://www.thehindu.com/news/national/central-vista-project-sc-dismisses-plea-against-delhi-hc-verdict-refusing-to-halt-work/article35031575.ece, accessed 17 December 2021.

[2] The Prime Minister's Citizen Assistance and Relief in Emergency Situations Fund (PM CARES Fund) was started on 27 March 2020. Since it is a public charitable trust chaired by the Prime Minister, it is not subject to audit by the Comptroller and Audit General of India. Questions were raised from different corners relating to the transparency of the fund. The plea for transferring funds received under it to the National Disaster Response Fund was declined by the Supreme Court. See Shruti Mahajan, 'No Need to Transfer COVID-19 Relief Money from PM CARES Fund, No Statutory Prohibition on Contributions to NDRF: Supreme Court', *Bar and Bench*, 18 August 2020, https://www.barandbench.com/news/litigation/no-need-to-transfer-money-from-pm-cares-fund-supreme-court, accessed 17 December 2021.

In a study mentioned earlier (in the introduction and chapter 5), David Landau and Rosalind Dixon say that 'it is not uncommon for judges to issue decisions that intentionally attack the core of electoral democracy'.[3] They make a global survey of constitutional courts giving unconstitutional directives to explain how 'previously independent courts can quite quickly and effectively become the enemies, rather than allies, of democracy'. The essay also helps us understand how governments of the day use the court to resolve serious political issues in a manner that suits them. India is not unfamiliar with a 'committed judiciary', as it was labelled during the Emergency. Today, there is no formal proclamation of Emergency under Article 352 of the Constitution. Yet, many get arrested and detained in prison on the basis of ostensibly untenable allegations. We live in a democracy of dangerous and deceptive illusions. You feel like you are living under a Constitution, whereas your sense of security ends the moment the government identifies you as an embarrassment to it.

An opaque system for selection of judges is at the root of the problem. After the collegium system evolved for the appointment of judges, the process is no longer democratic. By the end of 1998, the top court evolved a revised practice of Memorandum of Procedure in the appointment process, which enabled the executive to have a powerful say in the selection process. The invisible link of dependence, obedience and obligations can create newer threats to the functional autonomy of the judiciary. The existing space for post-retirement rehabilitation also poses a great challenge to judicial independence.

B.R. Ambedkar famously said that 'democracy is only a top-dressing on an Indian soil, which is essentially undemocratic'. The class character of the judiciary was a point raised by the veteran communist leader, E.M.S. Namboodiripad. The legal profession is extremely hierarchical. Star value is attributed to a few lawyers based on the money they earn or the proximity they have to power. A Reuters study that explained how a small number of elitist lawyers dominated the US Supreme Court[4] is a lesson for India.

Law is not an inscription in the abstract. The Supreme Court is

[3] David Landau and Rosalind Dixon, 'Abusive Judicial Review: Courts Against Democracy', *UC Davis Law Review*, vol. 53, 2020, pp. 1313–87, https://lawreview. law.ucdavis.edu/issues/53/3/53-3_Landau_Dixon.pdf, accessed 17 November 2021.

[4] Joan Biskupic, Janet Roberts and John Shiffman, 'The Echo Chamber: At America's Court of Last Resort, a Handful of Lawyers Now Dominates the Docket', A Reuters Special Report, *Reuters Investigates*, 8 December 2014, https://www.reuters.com/ investigates/special-report/scotus/, accessed 17 December 2021.

essentially a political institution, a centre of power. The judges selected, not elected, are supposed to take up a counter-majoritarian role. But left with no purse or sword, 'the least dangerous' branch of democracy, as Alexander Hamilton[5] famously put it, maintains a fundamental yet covert dependence on the executive and the legislature. The degree of independence varies with variations in political equations. *ADM Jabalpur v. Shivakant Shukla* (1976)[6] illustrated the dependence on the authoritative regime under Prime Minister Indira Gandhi. During weak coalitions at the centre, we have found a strong Supreme Court acting against corruption, environmental devastation and state excesses. But an overreaching executive with majoritarian impulses can try and maintain a weaker judiciary.

This dependence need not be strictly formal. In *Bijoe Emmanuel and Ors. v. State of Kerala and Ors.* (1986),[7] the top court held that Jehovah's Witnesses cannot be compelled to sing the national anthem for that could infringe their religious freedom. During 2016–18, the court on its own issued directives compelling the whole nation to stand up for the national anthem when played in cinema theatres. This reflects the populist ideas of nationalism overplaying the court's perceptions. As we shall see in chapter 18, judges, even off the bench, exhibit ideological inclinations which are *per se* unconstitutional.

The way the centre dominates the affairs of the nation today is different from the majoritarianism of yesteryears. High courts, because of the federalist character of the polity, are relatively less proximate to the powerful apparatus of a centrist state. But the Supreme Court exercises immense authority on political issues. Almost every significant legal battle in the realm of politics is ultimately adjudicated by it, as also administrative issues, ranging from the transfer of high court judges and enquiry against them. This cuts the roots of judicial federalism.

Granville Austin once had remarked: 'Equipped with the basic qualifications, attitudes, and experience for creating and working a democratic constitution, Indians did not default their tryst with destiny.'[8] Presently, we notice that as a people, we have defaulted in our tryst with destiny; the top

---

[5] Hamilton is regarded as one of the founding fathers of the United States who contributed immensely to the US Constitution.

[6] (1976) 2 SCC 521.

[7] (1986) 3 SCC 615.

[8] Granville Austin, *The Indian Constitution: Cornerstone of a Nation*, Oxford: Clarendon Press, 1966.

court is just a reflection of that. We are governed by a regime that does not believe in the ideology of the Constitution. When we fail in politics, we fail in law.

The Telegraph, 13 July 2021, https://www.telegraphindia.com/opinion/supreme-court-in-a-different-epoch-an-opaque-system-for-selection-of-judges-is-at-the-root-of-the-problem/cid/1786138.

11. A Court in Crisis

There was a long delay in appointing Justice K.M. Joseph as a judge of the Supreme Court in 2018 due to the centre's wilful reluctance. This poses serious questions relating to the unholy role that the executive played in the process, despite the collegium indicating its choice.

A COMMITTED JUDICIARY is a harsh Indian reality. Justice Khanna was denied elevation as the Chief Justice of India (CJI) because of his courage to state that the fundamental rights are inalienable even during the Emergency. However, the phenomenon of 'a committed judiciary' is not one that occurred only during the Emergency (1975–77), as is commonly understood. Even earlier, in 1973, three of the seniormost judges of the Supreme Court had to resign when they were superseded by a junior judge who was appointed as CJI. History repeated itself in a different fashion in the Justice K.M. Joseph episode. There was a delay of seven months before the centre approved the recommendation of the Supreme Court collegium to elevate Justice Joseph, then Chief Justice of Uttarakhand High Court, to the top court. Finally, on 7 August 2018, he took oath as a Supreme Court Justice.[1] A strong central government made its aggrandizing imposition on a weak and divided judiciary. Sometimes, political intrusion in judicial affairs has been an insurmountable tragedy in India.

The centre has no doubt exposed itself in not having a valid justification for turning down the collegium's recommendation to elevate Justice Joseph. Unlike the case of the elevation of a judge of the high court as chief justice of a high court, where seniority matters predominantly, for the elevation of a chief justice of a high court to the Supreme Court, seniority is not the sole criterion. This proposition has been unequivocally laid down by a nine-judge bench of the Supreme Court in the Presidential Reference Case (1998).[2] The apex court said that what matters for elevation to the Supreme Court is merit, not seniority. The primacy of the collegium and the finality of its unanimous

[1] 'Justices Indira Banerjee, Vineet Saran, KM Joseph Take Oath as Supreme Court Judges', *The Indian Express*, 7 August 2018, https://indianexpress.com/article/india/justices-indira-banerjee-vineet-saran-km-joseph-take-oath-as-sc-judges-5295364/, accessed 17 December 2021.

[2] (1998)7 SCC 739.

decision in the matter of appointment are also legal principles settled by the Supreme Court by way of the 2nd Judges Case (1993),[3] the 3rd Judges Case (1998)[4] and the relatively recent verdict in the *National Judicial Appointments Commission Case* (2015).[5]

Justice Joseph is an erudite judge, known for his intellectual ability and honesty. On 21 April 2016 he, along with Justice V.K. Bist, quashed the centre's order imposing President's Rule in Uttarakhand which was not preceded by a floor test in the Assembly. The judgement could not have been otherwise in view of the binding precedent in *S.R. Bommai v. Union of India* (1994),[6] in which the Supreme Court had mandated a floor test to ascertain the majority. Though the Supreme Court upheld the verdict, it resorted to a conciliatory approach in its order of 6 May 2016. Ultimately, it persuaded the centre to 'agree for a floor test', which reinstated the then Chief Minister Harish Rawat. The judgment of the High Court was more judicious. But merit often costs one dearly.

It is quite true that the moral authority of the Congress to question the centre is doubtful since it lacks democratic legitimacy in ensuring judicial independence in the past. The selection of judges by collegium, often based on a 'barter system' as revealed by Justice Chelameswar, is disgusting. Robert Stevens famously said: 'Judges choosing judges is the antithesis of democracy.'[7]

In the present scenario, 'merit' is a notion that is extremely abstract and obscure. Justice Chelameswar bemoaned that the elevation of judges to the top court is done based on impressions and not on evaluation. But the government and even the Supreme Court are bound by the nine-judge-bench ruling which remains the 'law of the land' by virtue of Article 141 of the Constitution. The centre's stand, expressed through the then Law Minister Ravi Shankar Prasad, also defied convention. A recent report showed that Justice Deepak Gupta of the Supreme Court was junior to more than forty-

---

[3] *Supreme Court Advocates-on-Record Association and another v. Union of India*, (1993) 4 SCC 441.

[4] In *Re: Presidential Reference*, (1998) 7 SCC 739.

[5] *Supreme Court Advocates-on-Record Association and Anr v. Union of India*, (2016) 5 SCC 1.

[6] (1994) 3 SCC 1.

[7] Robert Stevens, *The English Judges*, Oxford: Hart Publishing, 2002, p. 144, as cited in Alexander Horne, 'Is there a Case for Greater Legislative Involvement in the Judicial Appointments Process?', Study of Parliament Group, Paper No. 3, London, 2014, http://www.studyofparliament.org.uk/spg-paper-3.pdf, accessed 17 December 2021.

five judges in high courts across the country.[8] The same report showed that two judges of the Supreme Court from Karnataka, late Justice Mohan M. Shantanagoudar and Justice Abdul Nazeer, were junior to at least thirty-nine sitting high court judges.

The argument that Justice Joseph's elevation would result in over-representation for Kerala was fallacious. The only other judge from Kerala, Justice Kurian Joseph, was due to retire in November 2018. Curiously, 2018 witnessed many retirements as six judges vacated office that year. Thus, twelve vacancies were expected, as against the sanctioned strength of thirty-one in the apex court. This would have erased the putative anxiety of the centre about the inadequacy of regional or communal representation on the bench.

The process of appointments in constitutional courts in India still awaits a comprehensive legislation that encompasses all its facets. The very fact that the government can delay any appointment, as there is no statutory prescription of a time limit for approving or disapproving, is a sad commentary on the system. Justice Joseph's name was tied up in red tape and then 'returned' by the centre after an unjustifiable, inordinate and nefarious delay. Refusal to fill up judicial vacancies in the higher courts is nothing but an insult to the Constitution. An independent judiciary is a constitutional imperative, and a fair method for selection and elevation is its precedent condition.

Deccan Herald, 5 May 2018, https://www.deccanherald.com/specials/sunday-spotlight/even-supreme-court-not-spared-in-govt-demolition-drive-668458.html.

---

[8] Apurva Viswanath, 'Govt Opposes Justice Joseph's Elevation Due to Seniority, but Often Ignored it with Other Judges', *The Print*, 15 February 2018.

12. Transforming the Courts during the Pandemic

Virtual courts became indispensible during the time of the Covid-19 pandemic. The new system not only helped to resist the challenges of the pandemic, but also materialized the aspirations for quicker, easier, affordable access to justice for the masses at large.

AFTER THE SPREAD of Covid-19, both individuals and institutions began to behave differently. Distancing became the new rule. Amidst the pandemic, in the UK, the House of Commons met online for the first time. The Prime Minister of India interacted with Chief Ministers by video-conferencing. The Supreme Court of India and several high courts have heard many cases online. The Kerala High Court was a forerunner: on 30 March 2020, it passed orders on a few urgent matters; in a first, there was also live-streaming of the proceedings. Media reports clearly indicated the emergence of a different kind of judiciary.

Covid-19, which caught hold of the whole world, no doubt shocked the litigants, lawyers, judges and administrators of justice. Still, the coronavirus has the potential to recalibrate India's judiciary, provided we have the political will and an action plan to digitalize the courts, from the bottom to the top. The crisis can also be an opportunity.

Digitalization of the court is not merely about modernization. The point is its democratization. Technologists Eric Schmidt and Jared Cohen wrote: 'People will find that being connected virtually makes us feel more equal – its access to the same basic platforms, information and online resources – while significant differences persist in the physical world.'[1] To put it otherwise, digital technology offers formal equality. Substantive equality is quite another thing. The former can improve the struggle for the latter. It is fascinating to see a litigant in Chennai, with the assistance of his lawyer nearby, presenting his case before the Supreme Court through video-conferencing. Barriers of money, place, class and status are all demolished momentarily. British author Richard Susskind predicted that online courts are inevitable in times to come. Perhaps, the future is here.

The legal profession is deeply hierarchical. Many 'star lawyers' are beyond

---

[1] Eric Schmidt and Jared Cohen, *The New Digital Age: Reshaping the Future of People, Nations and Business*, London: John Murray, 2013.

the reach of the poor or even ordinary citizens. Judges also enjoy an elevated position, as physically visible in a conventional court hall. Access to justice is a myth for a good part of the population. In an open online court, everyone, right from the petitioner to the judge, from an outsider to the court staff, is in tiny rectangular spaces, reflecting the new digital equality – another variety of equality before the law stated in the Constitution. The problem in India, however, is that the internet too is the privilege of a few.

In a way, during the pandemic, the judiciary was materializing its own dream, as expressed in the judgment in *Meters and Instruments Pvt. Ltd. v. Kanchan Mehta* (2017),[2] which indicated that certain categories of cases 'can be partly or entirely concluded online'. Paperless methods can also reduce overcrowding in the courts, the judgment said. It is estimated that cases filed annually in the courts in India contain about 11 billion sheets, which ecologically means the destruction of lakhs of trees.

Digitalization can act as an effective remedy for the law's delays. In 1989, about one lakh cases were pending before the top court, which got reduced to 27,000 in 2003, thanks to computerization effected in 1990. By uploading documents ranging from the first information report in a local police station to the judgment of the Supreme Court on the website, the legal landscape of the country was radically altered. We have the basic platform to facilitate a digital revolution in our adjudicatory institutions. We need to learn from other jurisdictions as well. The online registry in the New South Wales Supreme Court, the Small Claims Tribunal (SCT) in Dubai and the Civil Resolution Tribunal (CRT) in Canada are fine examples. Singapore, China and South Korea also have good models to offer.

E-courts need proper, efficient and fair management. E-registries should be statutorily designed. They will have to function in accordance with rules specially promulgated. Timely allocation and utilization of funds should be ensured. A report by the Vidhi Centre for Legal Policy (2016) notes that policy-makers failed to properly estimate the cost of the e-courts project in India.

Virtual courts should however ensure the basic virtues of conventional judiciary. They should treat all lawyers alike. Citizens also should not be discriminated against. Principles of openness, fairness, transparency and accountability cannot be compromised. Barring a few complicated matters and elaborate trials, a good number of cases can be decided in e-courts hereafter. The interactive experiences should be satisfying and encouraging.

[2] (2018) 1 SCC 560.

There has to be a national policy in the matter that can take empirical lessons from the proceedings in different courts during the time of the pandemic.

A digital court has to be vibrant and participative. For that, the state should educate and equip the public. Acute poverty and illiteracy are antithetical to egalitarianism. Once we are able to resolve the feudal vices, the e-court can act as a check against monopolization of the facilities of Indian judicature. It can act against legal plutocracy. It can cultivate a new judicial culture for the people at large. It will, ideally, empower committed legal professionals across the country to extend efficient services to the needy at drastically reduced costs. It can help us move closer to a socialist judiciary and thereby, to the heart of the Constitution.

The New Indian Express, 2 May 2020, https://www.newindianexpress.com/opinions/2020/may/02/transforming-the-courts-during-pandemic-2138096.html.

13. Vocabulary of Justice in Our Country

Language connects the courts with the people. It also exposes the people who run the courts. We need to evolve a legal language that is simple, precise and communicative. Democratizing judgments is essential for democratizing the courts.

IN THE SEXUAL ABUSE case initiated by a law student against the former Union Minister Chinmayanand, while granting bail to the accused on 3 February 2020, Justice Rahul Chaturvedi of the Allahabad High Court opined that 'both of them used each other'. In the order, the relation between the woman complainant and the accused was termed as *'quid pro quo'* (one of mutual benefit) by the judge. It is significant to note that these findings occur in a bail order issued when the trial and adjudication were yet to happen. Findings on merit need to be avoided in an order granting or rejecting bail. In the instant case, Chinmayanand had been in custody since 20 September 2019 and the chargesheet also was filed. The judge, while granting bail, crossed the limits of judicial discipline and propriety with his unwarranted remarks.

The bail order reinstates the popular misunderstanding about the nature of the offence of rape by men in 'a position of authority' or having a fiduciary relationship with the victim, as stated in Section 376C of the Indian Penal Code. The order reinstates the patriarchal mindset. It also perpetuates sexual stereotypes that objectify a woman by blaming her for her silence. We are reminded of another rape case, *Tuka Ram v. State of Maharashtra* (1978),[1] in which the Supreme Court was widely criticized for finding fault with the silence of a young girl rather than the heinous offence committed by men on her. Lack of constitutional wisdom and patriarchy tell a sad commentary on our institutions.

The vocabulary of justice has, over the course of time, changed for worse. Many of us were disillusioned, quite justifiably, by the verdict of 9 November 2019 in the Ayodhya case[2] – for instance, when the top court talked about the 'Hindu side' and the 'Muslim side'. Legal scholar Andrew Goodman has illustrated the change in law's language. He indicates that the expression 'living

---

[1] (1979) 2 SCC 143.

[2] *M Siddiq (D) Thr Lrs v. Mahant Suresh Das and Ors.* (2010), Civil Appeal Nos 10866–10867.

in sin' was commonly used even in the 1980s, and later on, 'as a consequence of drastic social change', the judges had to evolve appropriate judicial terminology to deal with the property rights of unmarried cohabitees.[3] In India, the chairman of the Rajasthan Human Rights Commission described live-in relationships as a form of 'social terrorism' in 2017, despite the apex court's liberal view on the matter in *Khushboo v. Kanniammal* (2010).[4]

Brevity is no longer an accepted virtue in Indian courts, especially in constitutional cases. The verdict in *Kesavananda Bharati Sripadagalvaru and Ors. v. State of Kerala and Anr.* (1973),[5] which evolved the doctrine of the basic structure of the Constitution, ran into more than 700 pages. The verdict on the National Judicial Appointments Commission (2015), that spread over more than 1,000 pages, exceeded the size of the judgment in the *S.P. Gupta v. Union of India*[6] on judicial appointment (1981) that had roughly 830 pages. The Aadhaar judgment (2018)[7] had over 1,448 pages. Only very few even among lawyers would have read such verdicts in their entirety. On this, we have better lessons from other jurisdictions. The US Supreme Court's judgment in *Texas v. Johnson* (1989)[8] on free speech rights in the context of the right to burn the American flag had just forty-three pages. The verdict in *Lawrence v. Texas* (2003)[9] that decriminalized sodomy in the State of Texas had only forty-nine pages. *Roe v. Wade* (1973),[10] dealing with abortion rights,[11] had just 66 pages. The Brexit judgment delivered on 24 September 2019 by the UK Supreme Court[12] had just twenty-four pages. The constitution benches in the Indian Supreme Court can also adopt co-authorship in judgments to avoid repeated elaborations by each judge.

The language of the judgment also could sometimes lead to breach of

---

[3] Andrew Goodman, '*How Judges Decide Cases: Reading, Writing and Analysing Judgments*', Universal Law Publishing Co. Pvt. Ltd., first Indian reprint, 2007.

[4] (2010) 5 SCC 600.

[5] (1973) 4 SCC 225.

[6] (1981) Supp. SCC 87.

[7] *K.S. Puttaswamy and Anr v. Union of India and Anr.* (2017)10 SCC 1.

[8] 491 U.S. 397 (1989).

[9] 539 US 558 (2003).

[10] 410 US 113 (1973).

[11] In the US, many think that *Roe v. Wade*, that provided legal protection for lawful abortion, was not correct. This decision is now overruled. See https://www.cnbc.com/2022/06/24/roe-v-wade-overturned-by-supreme-court-ending-federal-abortion-rights.html, accessed 24 June 2022.

[12] See chapter 15.

peace. Shocked by the obscure verbosity in a Himachal Pradesh High Court judgment, a Supreme Court bench consisting of Justices Madan B. Lokur and Deepak Gupta set it aside and remanded the matter back to the High Court in 2017. The top court said that it was impossible to understand the judgment. A judgment written by the former Chief Justice of India Dipak Misra, in *Subramanian Swamy v. Union of India* (2016),[13] that challenged the criminal defamation law was also widely criticized for being incomprehensible.

Lawyer Michèle M. Asprey is the author of a work titled *Plain Language for Lawyers*.[14] In it, she advocates for radical changes in the lawyers' method of communication with the public, for according to her, lawyers are 'no longer seen as the learned custodians of unknowable secrets'. The principle should all the more apply to the literature from the bench.

Some, however, innocently think that the issue of bad judgments is only a matter of legal acumen, and that it can be resolved by judicial education and refresher courses. The merit of judgments has a direct correlation with the merit of judges. In the words of scholar Robert A. Leflar, 'The quality of our judges, and of their performance in the judicial process, is probably the surest guide to the quality of our civilisation.'[15] A good judgment needs to satisfy ethical, intellectual and aesthetic yardsticks. Dialogue with an informed bar is a processual imperative. Goodness of the judgment is to be taken as an extended goodness of the judge herself. Socrates warned that misuse of language induces evil in the soul. Therefore, our judges should definitely mind their language.

The New Indian Express, 13 February 2020, https://www.newindianexpress.com/opinions/2020/feb/13/vocabulary-of-justice-in-our-country-2102713.html.

[13] (2016) 7 SCC 221.

[14] Michèle M. Asprey, *Plain Language for Lawyers*, Delhi: Universal Law Publishing Co., first Indian reprint, 2002.

[15] Robert A. Leflar, 'The Quality of Judges', *Indiana Law Journal*, vol. 35, no. 3, pp. 289–305, p. 305, https://core.ac.uk/download/pdf/232657709.pdf, accessed 18 December 2021.

14. Compassion and the Court

Constitutional compassion could also be a judicial virtue. A close look at the Indian bench indicates erosion of this eternal value. This article registers concerns over the anger, anguish and exasperation from the bench, that have slowly and definitely replaced the fine feeling of mercifulness.

BARACK OBAMA, when he was the US president (2009–17), made a public statement on the appointment of judges to the US Supreme Court: 'I will seek someone who understands that justice isn't about some abstract legal theory or footnote in a case book; it is also about how our laws affect the daily realities of people's lives.' He said that the 'quality of empathy' is 'an essential ingredient for arriving at just decisions'.

The opinion ignited serious intellectual discourse. A few asked whether the President was pleading for a populist judiciary with moral rhetoric, and whether constitutional interpretation would become an extended form of politics. However, many others tried to perceive a symbiotic relation between compassion and the court in certain cases.

The connection between empathy and the law has all-time relevance. The court is no longer an unfamiliar area or a dangerous zone. The commoner wants to see it as a public place where human emotions do have a role. Ethical responsiveness is a human quality and therefore also a judicial virtue. As American philosopher Martha C. Nussbaum explained, 'Without its charity, reason is cold and cruel.' For Arthur Schopenhauer, compassion is the very foundation of morality. While explaining 'the unbearable lightness of being', Milan Kundera finds that 'there is nothing heavier than compassion' (*The Unbearable Lightness of Being*, 1984).

Compassion is not alien to the Indian courts or to the Constitution of the country. A closer reading of Article 51A (g) would signify this value in the fundamental law. While speaking about environmental protection, the Constitution motivates us 'to have compassion for living creatures'. In an ingenious judgment, Justice Bhagwati redefined the idea of *locus standi* (right to bring legal action) and said that a member of the public could approach the court on behalf of the helpless, disabled and the backward who are denied access to justice (*S.P. Gupta v. Union of India*, 1981).[1]

---

[1] (1981) Supp. SCC 87.

The Public Interest Litigation (PIL) movement in the country had multiple dimensions. It encompassed areas ranging from civil liberties to social justice. Anti-corruption struggles often had their litigative versions, which, however, were sometimes criticized for partisanship or lack of good faith. Very often, deterrence, aggression and hatred defined the social action litigations in the country. Reinstalling compassion at the heart of the PIL movement in India could be an important idea today.

In a few small villages in the northern part of Kerala, as a result of aerial spraying of the toxic pesticide Endosulfan between 1975 and 2000, thousands including newborns were fatally affected. Life became more difficult than death. It was an inter-generational calamity. Politicians, the media and social activists showed solidarity with the victims. Struggles on the street became the order of the day. Those struggles continued for almost a couple of decades.

Ultimately, on 10 January 2019, it took a single page for the top court to grant a substantial compensation of Rs 5 lakh to the victims after a writ petition was filed by the Democratic Youth Federation of India (DYFI). It was a gesture of compassion. The court, in that case, had to travel beyond the conventional limits of judicial review. It needed activists and humanists on the bench. Such judicial gestures are, however, relatively rare in recent times. One finds anger, anguish and exasperation on the bench, instead of empathy.

But social action litigation in India is criticized as a device that damaged the very institution of judiciary, especially in the post-Emergency phase.[2] Of late, PIL as an institution has lost its initial charm and modesty. It is often publicity-based or ill-motivated. Historically, however, one notices that the PIL has been a most formidable litigative device that humanized the Indian constitutional courts.

Since 1984, in a series of M.C. Mehta cases, the court backed a cleaner environment. Professor Upendra Baxi famously said in 1985 that the Supreme Court of India was becoming 'the Supreme Court for Indians' at the behest of judges like Justice V.R. Krishna Iyer and Justice P.N. Bhagwati.[3] Justice Iyer ruled consistently against handcuffing (*Prem Shankar Shukla*

[2] See Anuj Bhuwania, *Courting the People: Public Interest Litigation in Post-Emergency India*, Delhi: Cambridge University Press, 2017.

[3] Upendra Baxi, 'Taking Suffering Seriously: Social Action Litigation in The Supreme Court of India', *Third World Legal Studies*, vol. 4, 1985, pp. 107–29, https://scholar. valpo.edu/cgi/viewcontent.cgi?article=1125&context=twls, accessed 18 December 2021.

v. Delhi Administration, 1980),[4] solitary confinement (*Sunil Batra v. Delhi Administration*, 1979)[5] and imposition of onerous conditions for grant of bail (*Gudikanti Narasimhulu and Ors. v. High Court of Andhra Pradesh*, 1977).[6] The top court rescued the blinded undertrial prisoners of Bihar (*Hussainara Khatoon v. Home Secretary, State of Bihar*, 1979).[7] In *Samatha v. State of Andhra Pradesh and Ors.* (1997),[8] the court empathized with the tribals and said that they have a fundamental right to land. In the Asiad case (*People's Union for Democratic Rights and Ors. v. Union of India Ors,* 1982),[9] child labourers were given the solace of judicial activism. The court ordered compensation for illegal imprisonment in the Rudul Sah case (*Rudul Sah v. State of Bihar and Anr.*, 1983),[10] and the ground for damages was custodial death in the Nilabati Behera case (*Nilabati Behera v. State of Orissa and Ors.*, 1993).[11]

As time passes, we no longer have much of socialist jurisprudence. The courts, like other institutions, follow the rules of a globalized world. A juridical elitism is slowly coming into place. The concern, however, is not only about the erosion of socialist values or egalitarianism, but also about a process that invisibly annihilates humanism on the bench. The judges of the higher courts need to regain their power to perceive. We need another brand of advocacy in human tragedies. There are instances where the court needs to be simultaneously sympathetic and judicious.

The New Indian Express, 11 July 2019, https://www.newindianexpress.com/opinions/2019/jul/11/compassion-and-the-court-2002219.html.

[4] (1980) 3 SCC 526.
[5] (1980) 3 SCC 488.
[6] (1978) 1 SCC 240.
[7] (1980) 1 SCC 115.
[8] (1997) 8 SCC 191.
[9] (1982) 3 SCC 235.
[10] (1983) 2 SCC 141.
[11] (1993) 2 SCC 746.

15. Lessons from a Landmark Brexit Verdict

The UK Supreme Court's timely verdict on Brexit, by implication, emphasized the value of debate. It also upheld the importance of the legislature and asserted that the law-making body is not subservient to the executive. The verdict, which is clean and brief, offers a lot to countries like India in terms of understanding the potential of deliberative democracy.

THE UK SUPREME COURT pronounced its seismic judgment in *R (Miller) v. The Prime Minister*[1] on 24 September 2019. The court held that Prime Minister Boris Johnson's advice to the Queen to prorogue Parliament for about five weeks was unlawful. Suspension of Parliament precisely meant an abrupt detachment from the European Union (EU) by the end of October 2019, without Parliament being able to chart out an exit plan by formulating the terms or exercising other options.

Brexit involves enormous uncertainties for the citizens of the UK as well as other European countries. Johnson expected better advantages for Britain in negotiations with the EU. Many in Parliament, however, wanted predictability and certainty regarding the conditions of Brexit, so as to make the process less miserable and more humane. The Prime Minister's agenda was to invoke his 'executive prerogative' and to put a gag on Parliament. It suffered a judicial masterstroke. The protests in London endorsed the verdict in clear terms: 'Don't silence our MPs.'

Apart from its political connotations and implications for the public at large, the judgment is a triumph for constitutionalism across the world. The eleven-judge bench headed by Lady Hale said that the PM's action is justiciable and the question relating to legality of the advice to the Queen is not a forbidden zone for the court. It declared that sovereignty of Parliament, the first principle of the British Constitution, was diluted by invoking the prerogative power of prorogation.

According to the judgment, the executive (read, the Prime Minister) cannot 'prevent Parliament from exercising its legislative authority for as long as it pleased'. The court gave equal emphasis to the second principle of the UK's unwritten Constitution, namely, parliamentary accountability. It quoted Lord Bingham of Cornhill who laid down the legal position that

[1] (2019) UK SC 41.

'the conduct of Government by a Prime Minister and Cabinet collectively responsible and accountable to Parliament lies at the heart of Westminster democracy'. The court categorically held that 'the Prime Minister's action had the effect of frustrating or preventing the constitutional role of Parliament in holding the Government to account'.

The historic judgment has a few lessons to offer. The Indian Supreme Court in its landmark verdict in *Kesavananda Bharati Sripadagalvaru and Ors. v. State of Kerala and Anr.* (1973)[2] held that Parliament cannot, by way of amendment, alter the basic structure of the Constitution. There is a general perception that *R (Miller) v. Prime Minister*, in its own way, laid down the UK's 'basic structure' doctrine in a pernicious situation. The Indian judgment directed itself against executive and legislative excessiveness, whereas the UK verdict tried to forestall executive high-handedness and protect Parliament. The Indian judgment antagonized the then Prime Minister Indira Gandhi, who in turn effected the elevation of Justice A.N. Ray, who dissented from the majority view, as Chief Justice of India. In the process, three senior judges – Justices J.M. Shelat, K.S. Hegde and A.N. Grover – who ruled against the government were superseded. For sure, the judges of the UK Supreme Court did not face any such executive threat pursuant to the Brexit pronouncement.

Incidentally, as noted in chapter 13, the UK judgment has just twenty-four pages. Brevity and clarity are judicial virtues of universal value. The simple verdict was delivered quickly, as necessitated by the circumstances. The arguments were heard on 17, 18 and 19 September 2019, and the judgment was delivered within a week. Even an unconventional situation in the UK could be resolved with thoroughly conventional constitutional tools. The timely verdict decided the gravest constitutional issue in that nation's recent history. The failure of the Indian Supreme Court to act as the guardian of the Constitution in critical situations calls for honest introspection.

The UK verdict, by implication, emphasized the value of debates in the legislature. A deliberative democracy needs to recognize the potential of parliamentary debates, for it is the forum where people of the country talk to one another through their elected representatives. There is greater democratic legitimacy for decisions taken by Parliament than by the executive. This is, however, wishful thinking in the Indian context. A major part of productive time in both Houses of Parliament is notoriously wasted due to disruptions. We need to cultivate a responsible and pluralistic legislative morality.

There is nothing resembling a committed judiciary in the UK and that in

---

[2] (1973) 4 SCC 225.

itself is the foundational reason for the judgment which upheld that country's constitutional legacy. It therefore follows that an opaque, collegium-centred judicial system in India needs structural reforms to gain functional results.

The New Indian Express, 3 October 2021, https://www.newindianexpress.com/opinions/2019/oct/03/lessons-from-a-landmark-brexit-verdict-2042528.html.

16. Justice Gogoi: A Wrong Choice

Former Chief Justice of India Ranjan Gogoi has come out with an autobiographical work, Justice for the Judge. *The country, however, talks about the justice expected from judges. This article was written when Justice Gogoi was nominated to the Upper House of Parliament.*

JAMES C. SHEPPARD wrote an interesting essay on judicial retirement in the American context with the subtitle, 'The Age of Judges and the Judges of Ages'.[1] This subtitle attains relevance in a totally different context in India. Unlike in the US, the Constitution of India prescribes a formal retirement age for judges of the high courts and the Supreme Court – at 62 years and 65 years, respectively. In practice, somehow, judicial retirement in India is only a kind of metamorphosis to some other form – political, bureaucratic or administrative. Many judges in India, in effect, do not retire. Thus, in practice, we have many aged judges and only a few judges of ages.

The nomination of Justice Ranjan Gogoi as a Rajya Sabha member has created controversy. Many view it as a gesture of political favouritism. Such instances of post-retirement rehabilitation pose a great threat to the independence of the judiciary. But the idea is not altogether new. Justice Chagla, Chief Justice of the Bombay High Court, was appointed as a diplomat to the USA and to the UK by Prime Minister Jawaharlal Nehru. It was more a choice of the person than a political decision. Mohammad Hidayatullah retired as Chief Justice in 1970 and became the Vice President of India in 1979, which, however, was based on consensus.

There have been political games that were too obvious to be mistaken. Justice Baharul Islam resigned from the Rajya Sabha in 1972 to become a judge of the Gauhati High Court and after his retirement as Chief Justice of that court, he was made a judge of the Supreme Court. Later, he resigned from the Supreme Court to contest for the Lok Sabha as a Congress candidate. Chief Justice Ranganath Misra's berth in the Upper House of Parliament became controversial. The Commission he headed earlier had probed the anti-Sikh riots (1984) and exonerated the ruling Congress.

Political appointments of judges in India are therefore not unprecedented.

---

[1] James C. Sheppard, 'Judicial Retirement: The Age of Judges and the Judges of Ages', *American Bar Association Journal*, vol. 44, no. 2, February 1958, pp. 145–48.

There is also a long list of retired judges who were chosen as heads of statutory bodies like the National Green Tribunal, the Lok Ayukta, etc. Those appointments, however, had the backing of statutory prescription.

It is not unusual for a parliament to have certain nominated members from various walks of knowledge. Canada, Egypt, Ireland, Italy, the UK and other countries have adopted such practice.

POLITICAL NOMINATION

But unlike an appointment to the statutory bodies, a political nomination calls for stricter scrutiny. Article 80(3) of the Constitution empowers the President to nominate 'persons having special knowledge or practical experience' in matters such as literature, science and social service. A literal interpretation of Article 80 may include a person from the field of law as well within its ambit, on account of the use of the words 'such as'. The fields referred to are only illustrative and not exhaustive, as rightly held by the Delhi High Court in *Ram Gopal Singh Sisodia v. Union of India* (2012).[2]

This clause, however, has an ethical dimension. It is a constitutional encomium to those who have contributed to the nation and her people by virtue of their expertise. But mere knowledge or experience does not suffice. To say that any arbitrary and politically motivated decision without moral and judicious judgement would be protected by Article 80 is an amoral reading of the constitutional provision.

J.H. Proctor, in a 1985 essay, said that 'most of the 60 members nominated during the first 30 years [of the Republic] have been men and women of great artistic or intellectual attainment but no political experience'.[3] He also remarked that the nominated members 'were generally listened to respectfully' in the House. Between 1952 and 2013, some 119 persons were nominated to the Rajya Sabha, according to Subhash Kashyap.[4]

The centre and the President are legally and constitutionally entitled to make the nomination. But in the matter of Gogoi, the nomination lacked

---

[2] (2012) SCC OnLine Del 6310. In this case, the petitioner, Ram Gopal Singh Sisodia, challenged the nomination of cricketer Sachin Tendulkar to the Rajya Sabha. The High Court dismissed the plea as per its judgment of 19 December 2012.

[3] J.H. Proctor, 'The Nominated Members of India's Council of States: A Study of Role-Definition', *Legislative Studies Quarterly*, vol. 10, no. 1, February 1985, pp. 53–70.

[4] Subhash C. Kashyap, *Constitutional Law of India*, vol. 2, Universal Law Publishing, second edition, 2015.

legitimacy. On the bench, Justice Ranjan Gogoi defended himself and accused the complainant. Off the bench, in a press conference, he attacked the then Chief Justice. His double stand on post-retirement avocation is troubling.[5] The fact remains that the crucial questions about his nomination remain unanswered or wrongly answered even now, despite the series of TV interviews by the ex-judge.

It is the reactions of Justice Gogoi even more than the allegations against him that make him ineligible for the benevolence of Article 80(3). A system that creates and perpetuates an unholy nexus between the different branches of power is inherently partisan and undemocratic. The actions and omissions of Justice Gogoi will remain instructive and cautionary.

The Deccan Herald, 30 March 2020, https://www.deccanherald.com/opinion/in-perspective/unanswered-queries-ranjan-gogoi-s-choice-wrong-819062.html

---

[5] While hearing petitions concerning appointments to the tribunals on 27 March 2019, the then Chief Justice Gogoi opined that 'there is a saying that post-retirement appointment is itself a scar on the independence of the judiciary', and that 'it is a very strong viewpoint' (Tribunals CB [Day-1, Session-1). See Mehal Jain, 'There is a Strong View Point That Post-Retirement Appointments is a Scar on Independence of Judiciary, Says CJI', *Live Law*, 27 March 2019, https://www.livelaw.in/top-stories/tribunals-constitution-bench-day-1-session-1-143862?infinitescroll=1, accessed 20 December 2021.

17. A Supreme Court of Possibilities

At the end, one finds some rays of hope from the top court trying to assert itself against a powerful executive. But a lot of issues remain to be judicially tackled. Those include issues with the judiciary as well.

D URING THE PEGASUS case[1] hearing, the Supreme Court asked tough questions to the centre and reserved the matter for interim orders. The centre's unwillingness to file a proper affidavit and its bafflement over the question of whether they used Pegasus or not might invite the court's judicial opinion. A speculation on the final outcome is not the intent of this piece. Suffice to say that the case saw an assertive Supreme Court that rose above narrow interests and temporary political constraints. It remained serious about the allegation that national security was used as a ruse for snooping on the citizens and retaining power at any cost.

Apart from the Pegasus case, on and off the bench, Chief Justice Ramana made certain comments that reflected his sense of constitutionalism. Harish Khare, in a column, said that a 'Raman(a) Effect' was evident when the Chief Justice reminded the nation about the tyranny of elected majorities.[2] India has witnessed the perils of such majoritarianism during the Emergency (1975–77). It remains a constitutional alarm bell for the future.

An elected government could turn autocratic and try to annul the Constitution in various ways. As we have seen in earlier chapters, it can pass legislations that subvert the Constitution. It can withhold its purse and refuse to heed the requirements of the judiciary, ranging from human resources to infrastructure. It can impose its likes and dislikes upon the judiciary and thereby meddle with judicial appointments, elevations and transfers. It can woo the judges with offers of post-retirement rehabilitations. It can invoke its agencies and draconian laws against the dissenters and try to dismantle their judicial remedies.

The quality of democracy is indicated by the dialectical relation between the political wing and the judicial wing. Even the much-politicized judiciary in the US was unwilling to accept any of the challenges made to the electoral

---

[1] See chapter 35 for more on the Pegasus case.
[2] Harish Khare, 'The Ramana Effect: The 48th CJI Has Restored Judicial Spirit and Spark', *The Wire*, 17 September 2021, https://thewire.in/law/ramana-effect-supreme-court-judicial-spirit-spark, accessed 24 December 2021.

result that ousted the Trump administration. In the UK, as we noted in chapter 15, the Supreme Court, by way of its Brexit verdict (2019), set aside the Prime Minister's move to suspend the Parliament. In Sri Lanka in 2018, when the then President Maithripala Sirisena dismissed Prime Minister Ranil Wickremesinghe who enjoyed clear majority in the House and appointed Mahinda Rajapaksa as the PM, it was the Supreme Court that interdicted Rajapaksa from functioning as the premier, because of which Wickremesinghe was reappointed. This was how democracy was saved in the island nation.

These are a few instances where an assertive court could come to the rescue of the Constitution and the people in the Republic. But one would not be euphoric about the courts across the world on reading Landau and Dixon: 'Courts around the world, for example, have legitimated antidemocratic laws and practices, banned opposition parties to constrict the electoral sphere, eliminated presidential term limits and repressed opposition-held legislatures.'[3] In this empirical study, the authors explain how the constitutional courts are captured by the executive in different countries. In Venezuela and Hungary, laws were made to control the court, whereas in Bolivia, impeachment was used to tame the judiciary. History shows that in nations like Nicaragua, Russia and Pakistan, the court has endorsed the mischiefs of the political wing and ceased to be a fine arbiter.

The Indian judiciary is at a crossroads. During recent years, many cases of constitutional importance have not been heard by the top court in time. The plea against the sedition law or the Citizenship Amendment Act, and pleas challenging electoral bonds and the reorganization of Jammu and Kashmir in 2019 by taking away its special status, are pending adjudication. The validity of economic reservation by way of the 103rd constitutional amendment also awaits a decision. Special care needs to be taken to expedite the pleas for release of political prisoners in the country by whatever legal means possible. The Supreme Court needs to act as the first court of liberty, the Constitution's essential promise.

The Chief Justice can do a lot in bringing reforms into the system, as demonstrated by Willy Mutunga, former Chief Justice of Kenya, who activated ombudspersons to connect the court with the people. Chief Justice Ramana can continue and improve the online hearing system now evolved in the Supreme Court and ensure access to justice for the people of this vast

---

[3] David Landau and Rosalind Dixon, 'Abusive Judicial Review: Courts Against Democracy', *UC Davis Law Review*, vol. 53, 2020, pp. 1313–87, https://lawreview. law.ucdavis.edu/issues/53/3/53-3_Landau_Dixon.pdf, accessed 24 December 2021.

country. As explained in chapter 12, the inauguration of virtual courts in 2020 is perhaps the most significant transformation that has taken place in the Indian judicial system recently. As Justice D.Y. Chandrachud said, a change in the mindset among lawyers and judges is necessary to achieve the goal of paperless courts.[4]

There is great potential for enhancing the quality of the judicial system. Some suggestions include better judicial management, prioritizing the hearing of matters of imprisonment and deprivation of liberty, effective e-filing, speedy disposal of cases, female and minority representation among judges, and the expansion of virtual courts. Establishing regional benches of the Supreme Court in different parts of the country will go a long way in reducing pendency and improving judicial productivity. Dismantling the hierarchy between designated senior lawyers and others is also crucial to maintain a homogenous lawyer fraternity. Legal plutocracy in all its forms should be discouraged and fair advocacy encouraged. The crucial aspect, however, is to retain the independence of the judiciary and embrace its role as an effective counter-majoritarian institution in a democracy.

The New Indian Express, 24 September 2021, https://www.newindianexpress.com/opinions/columns/2021/sep/24/a-supreme-court-of-possibilities-2362853.html.

---

[4] Mehal Jain, 'Paperless Court Not Possible Without a Change in the Mindset of Bar and the Bench: Justice DY Chandrachud', *Live Law*, 12 September 2021, https://www.livelaw.in/top-stories/justice-dy-chandrachud-on-paperless-courts-digitisation-bar-and-bench-181424, accessed 24 December 2021.

18. An Unfortunate Ideological Shift in the Judiciary

Casteism in India has a long history. Indian society has been not only unequal, but exploitative. The Hindutva forces, however, talk about a 'magnificent' past in support of their hegemonic political agenda based on narrow nationalism. It is all the more worrying when a judge of the Supreme Court openly supports the call for legal revivalism. In this context, a talk by Justice S. Abdul Nazeer of the Supreme Court has serious legal and political connotations.

A SPEECH BY Justice S. Abdul Nazeer of the Supreme Court of India[1] has evoked a vibrant discourse in legal and political circles. The judge spoke in Hyderabad on the topic 'Decolonization of the Indian Legal System', at the National Council meeting of the Akhil Bharatiya Adhivakta Parishad, which is a lawyers' organization with express loyalty to the Bharatiya Janata Party (BJP). He called for 'Indianization' of our legal system. He lamented the continued neglect of the teachings of legal giants of ancient India such as Manu, Kautilya, Yajnavalkya, etc.

A 'LINK'

This apathy has been against 'our national interest', said the judge, adding that the kingdoms of ancient India had a fine justice dispensation system. He underlined Kautilya's theory about the duties of the king, which, according to him, is based on the great tradition established in the age of the *Ramayana*. He implied that many ideas of modern methods of adjudication were prevalent in indigenous jurisprudence.

While talking about judicial corruption, quoting Brihaspati, Justice Nazeer stated that 'a corrupt judge, a false witness and the murderer of a brahmin' could be considered as criminals on par with one another.

---

[1] Krishnadas Rajagopal, 'Supreme Court's Views on "Indianization" of the Legal System Have Varied', *The Hindu*, 29 December 2021. For more details and the full text of the speech, see Mehal Jain, 'Neglect of Ancient Indian Legal Giants Like Manu, Kautilya & Adherence to Colonial Legal System Detrimental to Constitutional Goals: Justice Abdul Nazeer', *Live Law*, 27 December 2021, https://www.livelaw.in/top-stories/justice-abdul-nazeer-ancient-indian-jurisprudence-manu-kautilya-colonial-legal-system-188437, accessed 9 January 2022.

Evidently, the brahmins remained on a different pedestal even while assessing the culpability of the act. On selection of judges, he recalled the Vedic priest Katyayana, who insisted that the king had to appoint only a brahmin to act as a judge. It is equally curious that Justice Nazeer has found glory in the *Artha-shastra*, which contemplated punishment for an official for personally talking with a woman employee during work hours.

The speech by Justice Nazeer has certain distinct characteristics. It is nostalgic in tone and abstract in its concept. It lacks coherence in terms of specific legal situations. The speech contained generalizations without situational references. It did not indicate a concrete and comprehensive legal system that is desirable or adaptable for the nation after independence. The basic problems with the speech, however, are two-fold. First, it ignores the Constituent Assembly debates on designing the nation's legal landscape. Second, when religious revivalism is used as a political tool by the ruling dispensation, the legal revivalism expounded by the judge in generic terms can only subserve the regime's political and populist agenda.

THE CONSTITUENT ASSEMBLY DEBATES

The Constituent Assembly debates started on 9 December 1946 and were completed on 26 November 1949, the day on which the Assembly approved the draft. Though the Government of India Act, 1935 was a major source for the constitutional script, the debates in the Assembly and their outcome made it a unique sociopolitical document.

The plea for Indianness was very prominent in the discourse. K. Hanumanthaiah, a member from Mysore, lamented: 'We wanted the music of Veena or Sitar, but here we have the music of an English band' (17 November 1949). Pandit Govind Malaviya's suggestion was to start the Preamble to the Constitution with the words, 'by the grace of Parameshwar, The Supreme Being, Lord of the Universe . . .'. Mahavir Tyagi emphasized regaining of 'spiritual freedom' and not just political freedom (27 December 1948). Lokanath Misra was anxious about 'the complete annihilation of Hindu culture' (6 December 1948). On the other hand, H.V. Kamath warned that the history of Europe during the Middle Ages was 'bloody', showing 'the pernicious effects that flowed from the union of Church and State' (6 December 1948). He said that 'if a State identifies itself with any particular religion, there will be rift within the State'. This was in sharp contrast with what Lokanath Misra said: 'If you accept religion, you must accept Hinduism as it is practised by an overwhelming majority of the people of India' (3 December 1948).

These remarks and many others only epitomize the large number of kaleidoscopic viewpoints that the Assembly chose to deliberate on. The plea for 'Indianization' was confronted not only with the values of western liberal democracy, but also with the finer parts of the Indian tradition that were organically incorporated into the Constitution.

The second facet of Justice Nazeer's speech has contemporary relevance and to understand it, we need to contextualize the opinion. The speech tries to create a narrative of a good old past without any convincing materials in support of it. This is totally in line with the right wing's political rhetoric which relies on unsubstantiated glories of the past by ignoring the injustices that prevailed. Justice Nazeer's remarks have come at a time when the regime is trying to subvert the Constitution and the idea of the rule of law in multiple ways. At a time when even legislations are being used as a means to shatter constitutional tenets such as secularism and federalism, the remarks of the Supreme Court judge against the alleged colonial nature of the legal system, which includes the nation's Constitution, are deeply disturbing.

Metrics and a Descent

The country's democracy has stooped to a new low in recent times. It went down the scale in the freedom index as well as hunger index. On 27 December 2021, *The New York Times* reported that 'in India, laws against religious conversions have been accompanied by mob violence'. Hate speech has become a prominent mode of articulation in the country, abetted by selective invocation or non-invocation of the penal laws. When the Constitution becomes the most effective tool against electoral autocracy, the speech by Justice Nazeer has had only an adverse impact on movements striving to restore the values of the Constitution. It is significant that even while attacking the colonialized legal system, Justice Nazeer did not find fault with the sedition law or such other draconian penal provisions, which are all colonial remnants.

It is unfortunate to see judges, even off the bench, advocating an ideology that is different from that of the Constitution. Such instances may go against the Bangalore Principles of Judicial Conduct (2002) talking, *inter alia*, about propriety in all the activities of a judge.

Against Separation of Powers

But in the Indian context, the ideological change that occurs in the institution of the judiciary and the persons running it is another fundamental factor that determines the quality of the judiciary and polity. The quintessential relationship between judicial ideology and political ideology was explained by J.A.G. Griffith in his classic work, *The Politics of the Judiciary* (1977).[2] Remarks made by the judges on and off the bench need to be analysed by positioning them against political situations. Some comments by the judges could be an expression of sheer personal admiration for the Prime Minister, as discernible in Justice Arun Mishra's speech of February 2020, where he described the Prime Minister as a 'versatile genius who thinks globally and acts locally'. In February 2021, Justice M.R. Shah said that Prime Minister Modi is a 'popular, loved, vibrant and visionary leader'. Both these comments do not augur well for our democracy since they are not in tune with the constitutional scheme of the separation of powers and expected judicial behaviour. Justice Nazeer's views indicate an unfortunate ideological shift in our judiciary.

The Hindu, 1 January 2022, https://www.thehindu.com/opinion/lead/an-unfortunate-ideological-shift-in-the-judiciary/article38083370.ece.

[2] J.A.G. Griffith, *The Politics of the Judiciary*, Manchester: Manchester University Press, 1977.

PART THREE

ON FREEDOM

19. India Does Not Need a Sedition Law

This article focuses on the legal aspects of the sedition law, and discusses its political and historical facets, which are crucial. It is pertinent to note that since the end of November 2021, several petitions challenging the law have been pending in the Supreme Court. In a significant development, on 11 May 2022, the Supreme Court issued an interim order that essentially prevented the use of Section 124A of the Indian Penal Code, as it was used. This article was written much earlier.

ON 6 MARCH 2020, a Supreme Court bench consisting of Justices A.M. Khanwilkar and Dinesh Maheshwari declined to entertain a plea seeking guidelines for the registration of criminal cases for sedition. The petition made a specific reference to an incident in Karnataka where a sedition case was framed against a few persons in charge of a school for staging a play. Many such cases have been filed across the country in recent times. Some of them relate to putting up banners or raising political slogans.

Section 124A of the Indian Penal Code (IPC) deals with the offence of sedition. It is a colonial provision. By virtue of Article 372 of the Constitution it continued to govern the citizens of India, and has not been repealed. Its misuse has been rampant. Its history is curious. Prior to independence, the law was invoked against Gandhi, Bal Gangadhar Tilak, Lala Lajpat Rai, Aurobindo, Annie Besant and Abul Kalam Azad among others. In the 'great trial' of 1922, Gandhiji had said about the law: 'I know that some of the most loved of India's patriots have been convicted under it. I consider it to be a privilege, therefore, to be charged under that section.' Though Nehru criticized the provision as 'highly objectionable and obnoxious', at no point of time did the Congress-led centre think of repealing it. During unjust political situations, illiberal regimes continued to misuse the law against their own citizens.

According to the provision, words or signs or visible representations that bring hatred or contempt towards the government amount to the offence of sedition. The maximum punishment is imprisonment for life. So the law's very vocabulary has a draconian effect, as it indicates that even a criticism of the government could be branded as seditious. The sedition law, on the face of it, is intimidating and undemocratic.

However, in *Kedar Nath Singh v. State of Bihar* (1962),[1] the Supreme Court upheld the constitutional validity of the provision with a significant rider, that 'comments, however strongly worded, expressing disapprobation of actions of the government, without exciting those feelings which generate the inclination to cause public disorder by acts of violence, would not be penal'.

The court emphasized that even a stringent criticism, written or spoken, 'will be outside the scope of the section'. The accused in that case was a leader of the Forward Communist Party, who spoke about 'revolution' that would establish 'a government of the poor and the downtrodden in India'. In *Balwant Singh v. State of Punjab* (1995),[2] the top court said that a casual raising of a slogan like 'Khalistan Zindabad', without any other act, cannot attract the charge of sedition. *Bilal Ahmed Kaloo v. State of Andhra Pradesh* (1997)[3] said that existence of an overt act is the decisive ingredient of the offence.

The emerging legal position is that where there is no incitement to violence, there is no offence of sedition. Certain statements or remarks by themselves cannot make out an offence unless they 'create disorder or have the pernicious tendency to create public disorder', to use a phrase from *Kedar Nath*. To meet the ends of justice, the provision must be scrapped by the top court or repealed by the legislature.

There is an ostensible ambivalence in *Kedar Nath*, as it abundantly warns against the dangers of textual reading and motivated invocation of the provision by the police or the government of the day. The judgment relied on the British genesis of the sedition law, whereas in Britain itself the law was abolished in 2010 as it was found unsustainable in the light of the Human Rights Act, 1998. In countries like New Zealand, the USA, Canada and Australia, sedition law has either been abolished or put to disuse. In Nigeria, the provision was judicially struck down in *Arthur Nwankwo v. The State* (1985).[4] The Indian law on sedition is dangerously overbroad and capable of 'trapping the innocent', and so vulnerable to constitutional scrutiny. Again,

---

[1] AIR 1962 SC 955. Kedar Nath, a leader of the Forward Communist Party, made a fiery speech calling for revolution in a public rally. He was charged with sedition (Section 124A IPC) and the offence of promoting enmity (Section 505[b] IPC). The court clarified that the speech did not amount to sedition, but rejected the challenge against Section 124A.

[2] (1995) 3 SCC 214.

[3] (1997) 7 SCC 431.

[4] (1985) 6 NCLR 228. Arthur Nwankwo published a book criticizing the government and the Governor of Anambra state. The court held that the charge of sedition is untenable in the light of the 1979 Constitution of Nigeria.

other provisions in the penal code dealing with offences against the state are adequate to achieve the object of protection of sovereignty. Sections 121, 121A and 122 of the IPC deal with the offence of waging war against the government of India. There are special enactments to deal with terrorism and other anti-national activities.

As such, the provision is a risky addition even from the state's point of view. Reports say that 48 cases of sedition were registered in 2014, and the number rose to 70 in 2018. There is reason to think that the trend got further accelerated thereafter. During the four years since 2015, though 191 cases for sedition were filed, trials were concluded only in 43 among them, leading to only four convictions. This revelation by the National Crime Records Bureau (NCRB) is testimony to the law's humiliating track record. During the UPA regime in 2011, hundreds of activists who protested against the nuclear power plant at Kudankulam were booked for sedition.

In a famous decision in *Texas v. Johnson* (1989),[5] the US Supreme Court said that even the right to burn the US national flag falls within the ambit of free speech, for, in the words of Justice Anthony Kennedy, 'it is poignant but fundamental that the flag protects those who hold it in contempt'. India, on the other hand, requires a minimum guarantee that those who are on the streets saluting the national flag and holding the Constitution in their hands are not labelled as criminals. Mark Twain has put it in perspective: 'Loyalty to the country always; loyalty to the government, when it deserves it.'

The New Indian Express, 12 March 2020, https://www.newindianexpress.com/opinions/2020/mar/12/india-does-not-need-a-sedition-law-2115553.html.

[5] 491 US 397 (1989).

20. The State Should Listen to Its Critics

This article deals with the misuse of Section 199(2) of the Criminal Procedure Code (CrPC) in the light of a judgment by the Madras High Court. This law, which is seldom discussed, is an imminent threat to journalistic freedom.

THE MADRAS HIGH COURT, on 21 May 2020, exonerated a group of journalists of the charges of defamation over certain reports. Justice Abdul Quddhose said that 'a public servant or a constitutional functionary must be able to face criticism', and that 'the state cannot use criminal defamation cases to throttle democracy'.

Section 199(2) of the Criminal Procedure Code (CrPC) is a curious law. It enables the state and its functionaries to utilize the office of the public prosecutor to move a written complaint to the court of session and to prosecute people, claiming that the President, the Governor or a minister is defamed. Previous sanction of the government is essential for such complaints.

The phrase 'defamation of a public functionary' is, to some extent, ironical. The text of the provisions needs deconstruction for a proper understanding of the offence. Section 499 of the Indian Penal Code (IPC) deals with the offence of defamation and the same offence is referred to in Section 199 of the CrPC. The second exception to the IPC provision says that expression of an opinion in good faith concerning the conduct of a public servant in his discharge of public functions or his character is not defamation. With this exception, the need to incorporate it in the CrPC and to arm the state with government machinery is indeed questionable. In cases of personal defamation, the concerned public functionary can move the court personally without the aid of Section 199(2). This is clear from Section 199(6) of the Code. Public functionaries are generally criticized for their public activities, which when done in good faith, is not defamation.

In *Subramanian Swamy v. Union of India* (2016),[1] the Supreme Court refused to strike down the provisions relating to criminal defamation, which in turn kept Section 199 alive. However, the Indian experience shows that Section 199 has been abused by the political executive from time to time to

---

[1] (2016) 7 SCC 221.

suppress dissent and stifle criticism. It is also pre-censorship in disguise. It has a chilling effect on whistle-blowers.

The argument that defamation should cease to be a criminal offence does not appear to be correct. As such, Sections 499 to 502 of the IPC have their own rationale and purpose. A private action for defamation by invoking penal provisions has justification in so far as it seeks to protect the individuals who are entitled to preserve their reputation. But the problem with Section 199 is that it conceives public functionaries under the state as 'defamable' and motivates them to repress the dissidents with the instrumentalities of the very same state. Here also, every use of the law becomes a misuse, for it lacks democratic legitimacy.

The High Court's admonition is a great stimulus to the free speech jurisprudence that badly needed it during the time of the pandemic. The verdict has lessons to offer for democracies across the globe during and after the pandemic. Studies indicate that more than a hundred regimes in the world declared a state of emergency in one way or another after the spread of Covid-19.[2] Free speech faces newer threats during the time of pandemic. The United Nations High Commissioner for Human Rights, Michelle Bachelet, openly warned against dispensations worldwide becoming illiberal and abusing emergency powers on grounds of medical exigencies.

The recent verdict also alerts the judiciary in India at a time when its top court is being critiqued widely for almost going back to the infamous *ADM Jabalpur* moment. It was in *ADM Jabalpur v. Shivakant Shukla* (1976)[3] that the Supreme Court, by a majority, held that the fundamental rights could be suspended during the Emergency, at the will of the political executive. On issues ranging from internet rights to the plight of migrant workers, the top court had remained insensitive at the most precarious times.

In India, free speech faces several challenges. Even an innocent tweet, comment or speech is taken as the basis for booking people in different states, irrespective of the party in power. Political leaders, public activists, journalists, students, writers and cartoonists are targeted. Politics based on such first information reports (FIRs) is essentially undemocratic. In many

---

[2] Covid-19 Civic Freedom Tracker, Collaborative Effort by International Centre for Not-for-Profit Law, European Centre for Not-for-Profit Law, and UN Special Rapporteur on the promotion and protection of human rights and fundamental freedoms while countering terrorism, available at https://www.icnl.org/covid19 tracker/, accessed 2 December 2021.

[3] (1976) 2 SCC 521.

such cases, instead of Section 199 of the CrPC, governments use other devices in the IPC. There are outdated laws dealing with sedition (Section 124A) or blasphemy (Section 295A) that are misused. The nation needs a liberal reformative agenda to do away with such obsolete remnants of the colonial regime.

Potential for misuse is not a legal ground to strike down the law (*Shreya Singhal v. Union of India* [2015]).[4] But a law can be annulled if it is unconstitutional. The ethos of the Constitution is non-negotiable. Therefore, it is vital to ensure that freedom of speech is not unreasonably curtailed even during a state of emergency – financial, political or health-related. The European Court of Human Rights has laid down the correct proposition: 'Freedom of expression . . . is applicable not only to "information" or "ideas" that are favourably received or regarded as inoffensive or as a matter of indifference, but also to those that offend, shock or disturb the State or any sector of the population' (*Handyside v. United Kingdom* [1976]).[5]

The New Indian Express, 1 June 2020, https://www.newindianexpress.com/opinions/2020/jun/01/the-state-should-listen-to-its-critics-2150582.html.

---

[4] (2015) 5 SCC 1. Petitions were filed before the Supreme Court seeking to strike down Section 66A of the Information Technology Act, 2000. Section 66A concerns punishment for sending offensive messages by digital means. It has penalized such messages for 'causing annoyance, inconvenience, danger, obstruction, insult, injury', etc. The provision was held to be overbroad and unconstitutional as it curtails freedom of expression guaranteed under Article 19(1)(a) of the Constitution. Incidentally, it was laid down that potential for misuse is not a ground to strike down the law.

[5] (1976) ECHR 5.

21. Free Speech and the Judicial System

Courts are supposed to check excesses of the executive and legislative which curtail the freedom of speech and expression. What if the Supreme Court itself curtails freedom? This article was written in the wake of observations made by a bench led by Justice Arun Mishra while dealing with a contempt case against the lawyer Prasanth Bhushan.

POLITICIANS AND ADMINISTRATORS often resort to a convenient response to inconvenient questions, by saying that the topic referred to is *sub judice* (pending before the court), and that therefore they will not be able to comment on it. Lorne Sossin and Valerie Crystal, academics at York University, addressed such situations when they asked, 'Why should the existence of litigation excuse representatives of government from accounting for their and the government's actions?'[1]

In modern times, the courts in very many democracies are no longer doing their conventional functions alone. A clear shift from an adjudicatory job to an administrative role is visible in several jurisdictions. The situation in the US is illustrative of this. Jurist Ronald Dworkin said, 'In England, for example, the issue of whether minimum wage legislation is fair was a political issue, but in America it was a constitutional, that is, judicial issue as well.'[2]

As in the US, in India too, many political affairs become legal or constitutional matters, and as a result, the Indian Supreme Court, described as the most powerful court in the world due to its wide authority for judicial review, has become a formidable political power centre. Topics ranging from reservation to taxation and from temple entry to prohibition are ultimately decided by the country's top court.

A bench of the Supreme Court consisting of Justices Arun Mishra and Naveen Sinha, on 6 February 2019, came down heavily on the conduct of certain lawyers criticizing the judges and judiciary even as their cases await adjudication. The bench stated that the 'judiciary has to be protected from outside', and that 'some lawyers seem to be carrying a dagger to kill the judiciary'.

---

[1] Lorne Sossin and Valerie Crystal, 'A Comment on "No Comment": The Sub Judice Rule and the Accountability of Public Officials in the 21st Century', *Dalhousie Law Journal*, vol. 36, no. 2, 2013, pp. 535–80.

[2] Ronald Dworkin, *Taking Rights Seriously*, London: Bloomsbury Academic, 2013.

The exasperation has its own justification. The assertions by Lord Hardwicke in *Roach v. Garvan* (1742)[3] that 'nothing is more incumbent upon courts of justice than to preserve their proceedings from being misrepresented' has an institutional rationale. But preservation of procedural integrity cannot take a dictatorial form so as to gag 'argumentative Indians' including lawyers talking politics or the law. The quality of deliberation on judicial selection, Aadhaar, the adultery law, rights of transgender persons, etc., that happened in the responsible media was in no way inferior to the level of discourse that occurred in the court. Many a judgment of the Supreme Court on constitutional issues has profusely quoted from pieces that the media carried even during the course of litigation.

'Public discussion' is therefore a political duty, as famously put by Justice Brandeis. We have, in India, a flawed system for the appointment of judges, which even the apex court has acknowledged in its judgment on the National Judicial Appointments Commission (2015).[4] Robert H. Bork, a famous appeals court judge from the US, put the issue in perspective: 'Anyone who wants a decent, democratic government ought to be concerned about judges who misbehave, or exceed their authority or issue unjust decisions.'[5] The point, however, is not that anything is justified in the name of free speech. *Sub judice* may be a principle still relevant when it acts as a device to protect the rights of an individual or an accused.

Trial by media is a menace that needs correctional measures by way of appropriate self-regulations. The Supreme Court in *Sahara India Real Estate Corp. Ltd. and Ors. v. Securities and Exchange Board of India and Anr.* (2012)[6] and a full bench of the Kerala High Court in *S. Sudin v. The Union of India and Ors.*(2014)[7] laid down the same principle. Journalists and lawyers need

---

[3] (1742) 2 Atk 469.

[4] Though the Constitution provides for consultation by the executive with the Chief Justice for selecting the judges of the constitutional courts, the Supreme Court essentially held that judicial appointments can be done only with the concurrence of the Chief Justice and the collegium headed by him. This position was laid down in the Second Judges Case (1993) and the Third Judges Case (1998). There is no independent commission to select judges of the higher judiciary in India, nor is there a transparent process for the same. Thus, it is not uncommon to have controversial figures chosen to the high bench.

[5] Robert H. Bork, 'Foreword', in Max Boot, *Out of Order*, New York: Basic Books, 1998.

[6] (2012)10 SCC 603.

[7] 2014 SCC OnLine Ker 21351.

to act conscientiously while the matter involves a possibility to harm others.

As in the UK, the rule of *sub judice* in India is substantially codified in the Contempt of Courts Act, 1971. It however spares fair and accurate reporting of court proceedings and fair criticism of judgments from the clutches of the law. Whether a particular 'attack' on a court or a judge is offensive would therefore call for a legal scrutiny on a case-to-case basis, by referring to the existing laws. When there are enactments governing the field and providing for punishment, a judicial legislation is impermissible, as held by the apex court in *Supreme Court Women Lawyers Association v. Union of India* (2016).[8] A general gag order by the court, which would amount to pre-censorship, can be antithetical to the tenets of deliberative democracy. In the digital world of social media where each individual becomes a mobile republic, how far the courts can control expressions is another question. Fair criticism about the deficits or bias in an investigation – for example, the investigation by the police into the Delhi riots (2020) – should not be curtailed on the ground that the matter is pending adjudication.

By virtue of Article 19(2) of the Constitution, reasonable restrictions can be imposed only by a 'law' made by the state for certain specified purposes, which include laws 'in relation to contempt of court', 'incitement to an offence', etc. The country has such laws in abundance. Restraint by the judiciary in controversial matters alone would meet the requirements of a liberal polity. As Justice La Forest of the Supreme Court of Canada put it, 'the ability of a jury to disabuse itself of information that it is not entitled to consider is a great judicial virtue'.

The New Indian Express, 20 February 2021, https://www.newindianexpress.com/opinions/2019/feb/20/free-speech-and-the-judicial-system-1941197.html.

---

[8] (2016) 3 SCC 680. The Women Lawyers' Association moved the Supreme Court for suggesting to the Parliament to enhance the punishment for rape of girls under the age of sixteen, 'so that the legislature can appositely respond to the collective cry'.

22. Freedom in the Time of Covid-19

The Covid-19 pandemic has posed civilizational questions to the entire planet and its inhabitants. These include issues of freedom, equality and justice. This piece was written during the initial period of the contagion. The later phase involved more devastating scenes, as we shall see in chapter 36, 'Governance During the Pandemic'.

ALBERT CAMUS' NOVEL *The Plague* is a lesson for the human race on values – social, moral and political. It is often seen as an allegory for the political plague of Nazism that invaded France. It also vividly describes the gravity of the loss of life caused by the pandemic. Across the world, a big calamity can have a tendency to make the state stronger and the people weaker. The present infestation is no exception.

Along with the miseries that the virus has brought, the plight of migrant workers, household workers, rag pickers, daily wagers, street vendors and other marginalized sections among the workforce has now become part of the political discourse. The Supreme Court on its own cannot set right the problem. Let us take a look at the relevant laws. The country had promulgated the Inter-State Migrant Workmen (Regulation of Employment and Conditions of Service) Act way back in 1979. It stipulates registration of establishments where such workers are employed. There are provisions for the licensing of contractors. The Act also provides for adequate wage rates, displacement allowance, journey allowance, etc., along with other facilities. Section 16 of the Act guarantees just and reasonable pay, suitable residential accommodation and free medical aid. Non-compliance with the provisions could invite penal consequences.

The country also designed the Unorganized Workers' Social Security Act in 2008, with the laudable objective of providing a better quality of life for workers in the informal sector. It speaks about schemes to be designed by the central and state governments to improve the habitats of the proletarians.

These legislations were not only breached but even forgotten by the governments at the centre and states. The radical provisions of the statutes remained a non-starter. Had it been otherwise, and had there been imaginative preparatory measures before the inevitable lockdown, the labour scenario would have been different. The moving sight of populations of workers on the street once more evoked Camus' prophetic words: 'No longer were there individual destinies; only a collective destiny, made of plague . . .'.

'Stay at home' is a hollow rhetoric for many Indians who do not have a home. The Census of 2011 revealed that there are more than 17 lakh homeless people in our nation. Right to housing has been recognized as a fundamental right in a few modern constitutions (for example, Section 26 of the South African Constitution).[1] In India, right to property is no longer a fundamental right, as Article 19(1)(f) was deleted from the Constitution with effect from 20 June 1979. Today, it is at best a constitutional right as per Article 300A of the Constitution, which says that persons should not be deprived of property except by authority of law. This constitutional silence about an enforceable right of residence was sought to be indemnified to some extent by parliamentary legislations. The efforts, however, met with executive apathy, due to which the country now pays a hefty cost.

As Professor Frank M. Snowden of Yale University demonstrates in his scholarly work, *Epidemics and Society: From the Black Death to the Present* (2019),[2] a pandemic can lead to an illiberal regime and excessive exercise of power over the citizens. During the contagion, the right to privacy is curtailed to a considerable extent as its infringement is often justified in terms of a public health emergency. Control over the media is also on the state's agenda. Journalists have been booked for reporting the misdeeds of persons holding power. There are also instances of human rights violations. During such hard times, free flow of factual information and reports needs to be ensured.

The lockdown and other executive measures in India are backed by the Epidemic Diseases Act of 1897 and the Disaster Management Act of 2005. These statutes contain penal provisions and equip the authorities to deal with offending individuals. Section 3 of the 1897 statute makes disobedience of orders issued under the said Act punishable under Section 188 of the Indian Penal Code. Obstructions to relief activities, false claims, false warnings, etc., are punishable under Chapter 10 of the 2005 statute. The 1897 Act, which was made by the British in the background of the bubonic plague outbreak, is not wholly adequate to meet the requirements of today's globalized India.

---

[1] Section 26. Housing: 1. Everyone has the right to have access to adequate housing. 2. The state must take reasonable legislative and other measures, within its available resources, to achieve the progressive realization of this right. 3. No one may be evicted from their home, or have their home demolished, without an order of court made after considering all the relevant circumstances. No legislation may permit arbitrary evictions.

[2] Frank M. Snowden, *Epidemics and Society: From the Black Death to the Present*, The Open Yale Courses Series, New Haven: Yale University Press, 2019.

Article 257 of the Constitution empowers the Union to exercise control over the states during certain exigencies, but it does not alter the character of cooperative and collaborative federalism, a basic feature of our fundamental law. The centre would do well in taking all the states into confidence in our endeavour for survival.

It is not enough to impose the rigour of law on the public. The challenge is also to realize the law's humane face. The right to life, which means dignified life, has the protection of Article 359 of the Constitution, which says that it cannot be taken away even by a proclamation of Emergency. This was a significant constitutional correction done by the Janata regime under Morarji Desai by way of the 44th Amendment Act, 1978. It is the indignity attached to poor Indians that has got exposed during the days of the pandemic. For them, Article 21, speaking about the right to life, became *non est*.

The freedoms under Article 19 also became redundant. As Amartya Sen demonstrates in his celebrated book, *Development as Freedom* (1999),[3] poverty is understood as deprivation of the real freedom. Poverty is not merely the poor man's problem. National solidarity is an imperative to fight the virus and in the battle, the constitutional values of justice, liberty, equality and fraternity can have a catalytic effect.

The New Indian Express, 8 April 2020, https://www.newindianexpress.com/opinions/2020/apr/08/freedom-in-the-time-ofcovid-19-2127186.html.

---

[3] Amartya Sen, *Development as Freedom*, USA: Alfred A. Knopf, 1999.

23. P. Chidambaram: Beyond Jail and Bail

Former Union Minister and senior lawyer P. Chidambaram had to spend 106 days in prison after the courts repeatedly denied him bail. The episode illustrates the reluctance on the part of the courts to bat for liberty, even in cases where political vendetta is writ large. Democracy has a lot to learn from the case. Even today, the case has not been tried. The long pre-trial incarceration poses serious questions about our idea of liberty.

'FREEDOM IS INDIVISIBLE', P. Chidambaram said, quoting Nelson Mandela's famous words, after being released from Tihar Jail on 4 December 2019. He said only good things about the courts, though he was actually not treated well by the Delhi High Court or by the Supreme Court.

The belated grant of relief does not mitigate the gravity of the institutional failure that occurred in the episode. It is no longer a matter of the egregious folly of the Delhi High Court order declining bail to the former minister. It is also about the lack of intervention by the Supreme Court at the earliest occasion when it could have acted lawfully and constitutionally to protect the liberty of the aged citizen. In that case, the unnecessary incarceration for more than 100 days even after custodial interrogation could have been avoided or at least reduced.

The judgment authored by Supreme Court Justice A.S. Bopanna is however significant inasmuch as it lays down the correct principle of law. It reminded the courts about the conventional test to be applied while considering a bail application. In the bail petition, the courts only need to see whether the accused (1) may abscond; (2) may attempt to tamper with evidence; and (3) may try to influence the witnesses.

The first information report (FIR) in Chidambaram's case is late by a decade, and it rests on the fragile testimony of an approver, Indrani Mukerjea, whose credentials are yet to be tested in the trial. The high drama in which Central Bureau of Investigation (CBI) officers scaled the walls of the parliamentarian's residence was only the beginning of episodes that followed. The CBI and the Enforcement Directorate (ED) acted in synergy so as to prolong the detention.

In advanced democracies, parliamentarians possess immunity from arrest except in certain rare and justifiable situations. This is essentially a protection from political vendetta by the persons in power. Article 46 of the German Basic Law is an example.[1]

Woodrow Wilson famously said, 'the history of liberty is a history of the limitations of governmental power, not the increase of it'. But Indian history shows that the judiciary could seldom correct the illiberal atrocities of an aggrandizing state. Legal scholar Vincent Blasi has described 'pathological periods' in history when a mighty state would punish dissidents even 'for what they say or believe'.[2] A war or an Emergency can create such a danger zone.

One can have a different opinion about Chidambaram as a political leader. The way in which he used his power needs critical exposure. Perceptions may vary from person to person. But he always remained an erudite member of the bar whose advocacy is built upon intellectual strength and will power. His submissions in the money bill-related part in the famous Aadhaar case in 2018 were notable. He was clear, calm, focused and excellently streamlined in his arguments before the constitution bench of the top court led by Justice Dipak Misra. His son was under detention when he addressed the court.

The Supreme Court, in its last order granting bail, has correctly found fault with the practice of institutions relying on documents in a sealed cover to which others do not have access. The proceedings in a court cannot be reduced to a private affair. However, the top court ought not to have gagged the parliamentarian from making any comment on the case. He has the constitutional right to say that the action of the present regime is politically motivated.

---

[1] Article 46 [Immunities of Members] of the German Constituion lays down the following: (1) At no time may a Member be subjected to court proceedings or disciplinary action or otherwise called to account outside the Bundestag for a vote cast or a remark made by him in the Bundestag or in any of its committees. This provision shall not apply to defamatory insults. (2) A Member may not be called to account or arrested for a punishable offence without permission of the Bundestag unless he is apprehended while committing the offence or in the course of the following day. (3) The permission of the Bundestag shall also be required for any other restriction of a Member's freedom of the person or for the initiation of proceedings against a Member under Article 18. (4) Any criminal proceedings or any proceedings under Article 18 against a Member and any detention or other restriction of the freedom of his person shall be suspended at the demand of the Bundestag.

[2] Vincent A. Blasi, 'The Pathological Perspective and the First Amendment', *Columbia Law Review*, vol 85, no. 4, April 1985, pp. 449–514, https://scholarship.law. columbia.edu/cgi/viewcontent.cgi?article=1008&context=faculty_scholarship, accessed 18 December 2021.

In the 1970s, the American musician Bob Dylan's famous song 'Hurricane' accused the police, and even the court, of convicting boxer Rubin Carter for an alleged triple murder in 1967 based on racial prejudice and not legal evidence. It was at that time regarded as an improper and unlawful gesture of the great singer. Ultimately, after Carter's prolonged detention, in the retrial, the courts found that the conviction was wrong and not supported by legal evidence.

The gag order issued against Chidambaram, which even otherwise is unprecedented and unconstitutional, cannot stand the test of legitimacy since exoneration in the future is quite possible. It is ironic that in the present judgement the court correctly relied on the principles in *Gurbaksh Singh Sibbia etc. v. State of Punjab* (1980),[3] which, based on earlier case laws, said that 'an accused person who enjoys freedom is in a much better position to look after his case and to properly defend himself than if he were in custody'. *Sibbia* further said, 'As a presumably innocent person, [one] is . . . entitled to freedom and every opportunity to look after his own case. [He] must have his freedom to enable him to establish his innocence.'

As a matter of law, the same principle applies to an application for anticipatory bail. In *Siddharam Satlingappa Mhetre v. State of Maharashtra and Ors.* (2010),[4] the court relied on the *Sibbia* judgement to say that a special case need not be established for anticipatory bail, and that 'arrest should be the last option and it should be restricted to those exceptional cases where arresting the accused is imperative in the facts and circumstance of that case'. But the Supreme Court could not apply the principle at the pre-arrest stage in Chidambaram's case.

The practice of the courts, including the High Courts, of writing lengthy orders in sensational cases also requires to be criticized. It was almost uniform practice about a decade ago to grant or deny bail with a short order, with legal reasoning. Brevity is also a judicial virtue that helps to avoid an unwarranted analysis of the merit of the case at the pre-trial stage.

Let us not, however, reduce the episode to a mere legal question concerning jail or bail. It is essentially a political issue with an immense impact on the country's democracy.

Deccan Herald, 8 December 2019, https://www.deccanherald.com/opinion/main-article/p-chidambaram-beyond-jail-and-bail-783828.html.

[3] (1980) 2 SCC 565.
[4] (2011) 1 SCC 694.

24. A New Jurisprudence for Political Prisoners

A judgment of the Supreme Court of India on 28 October 2021 has immense potential to reclaim the idea of personal liberty and human dignity. In Thwaha Fasal v. Union of India,[1] the court has acted and demonstrated introspective jurisdiction and deconstructed the provisions of the Unlawful Activities (Prevention) Act (UAPA) with a great sense of legal realism. This paves the way for a formidable judicial authority against blatant misuse of this draconian law, dealt with in chapter 4.

THE BACKGROUND

IN THIS CASE from Kerala, as per the verdict of the Supreme Court, there are three accused, one of them absconding. The police registered the case and later the investigation was handed over to the National Investigation Agency (NIA). The accused were in their twenties when arrested on 1 November 2019. During the investigation, some materials containing radical literature were found, which included a book on caste issues in India and a translation of the dissent notes written by Rosa Luxemburg to Lenin. There were also leaflets that were allegedly related to Maoist organizations.

Thus, the provisions of the UAPA were invoked. Against the first accused, Allan Shuaib, offences under Sections 38 and 39 of the UAPA and 120B of the Indian Penal Code (IPC) were alleged. Section 38 deals with 'offence relating to membership of a terrorist organization' and Section 39 with 'offence relating to support given to a terrorist organization'. Section 120B of the IPC is the penal provision on criminal conspiracy. Against the second accused, Thwaha Fasal, over and above these charges, Section 13 of the UAPA was alleged – which is the provision about punishment for unlawful activities. Both the accused were students and there were no allegations of any overt act of violence. According to the accused, the charges were an attempt to label them as terrorists based on intellectual and ideological inclinations attributed to them.

[1] 2021 SCC OnLine 1000.

JUDICIAL TRAJECTORY

The case had a curious trajectory. After initial rejection of the pleas, the trial judge granted bail to both the accused in September 2020. By that time, the students had completed more than ten months in prison. The High Court, in appeal, while confirming Allan's bail, chose to set aside the bail granted to Thwaha. The matter then reached the Supreme Court. The Supreme Court, after a comprehensive examination, upheld the trial judge's finding that the materials, *prima facie*, do not show any 'intention on the part of both the accused to further the activities of the terrorist organization'. It found fault with the High Court for not venturing to record, *prima facie*, findings regarding charges against Thwaha, whose bail was set aside by the High Court. The top court confirmed the bail granted to both. Now, they have been set free.

The Supreme Court was emphatic and liberal when it said that mere association with a terrorist organization is not sufficient to attract the offences alleged. Unless and until the association and support were 'with intention of furthering the activities of a terrorist organization', offence under Section 38 or Section 39 is not made out, it said. Mere possession of documents or books by the accused at a formative young age, or even their fascination for an ideology, does not *ipso facto* or *ipso jure* make out an offence, the court ruled.

The judgment can act as effective admonition against a suppressive regime. It also exposes the hypocrisy of the UAPA law (see chapter 4). Section 43D(5) of the UAPA says that for many of the offences under the Act, bail should not be granted if, 'on perusal of the case diary or the report (of the investigation) . . . there are reasonable grounds for believing that the accusation . . . is *prima facie* true'. Thus, the Act prompts the court to consider the version of the prosecution alone while deciding the question of bail. Unlike the Criminal Procedure Code, the UAPA, by virtue of the proviso of Section 43D(2), permits keeping a person in prison for up to 180 days without even filing a charge sheet. Thus, the statute prevents comprehensive examination of the facts of the case, on the one hand, and prolongs the trial indefinitely by keeping the accused in prison, on the other. In chapter 4, we have seen how the Delhi High Court has dealt with this provision.

PRESUMPTION OF GUILT

Instead of presumption of innocence, the UAPA holds presumption of guilt of the accused. Section 43E of the Act expressly talks about 'presumption as to the offences'. According to Section 43D(5), jail is the rule and bail is often not even an exception. The court, in *Thwaha Fasal*, refused to construct this Section in a narrow and restrictive sense. This analysis has to some extent liberalized an otherwise illiberal bail clause. In the process, the court also tried to mitigate the egregious error committed by a two-judge bench of the Supreme Court in *National Investigation Agency v. Zahoor Ahmad Shah Watali* (2019)[2] that interpreted the same provision.

In *Zahoor Ahmad Shah Watali*, the court said that by virtue of Section 43D(5) of UAPA, the burden is on the accused to show that the prosecution case is not *prima facie* true. The proposition in *Zahoor Ahmad Shah Watali* is that the bail court should not even investigate deeply into the materials and evidence, and should consider the bail plea primarily based on the nature of the allegations, for, according to the court, Section 43D(5) prohibits a thorough and deeper examination. As such, in several cases bail pleas were rejected relying on *Zahoor Ahmad Shah Watali*, despite strong indications that the evidence itself was false or fabricated. Many intellectuals including Sudha Bharadwaj and Siddique Kappan were denied bail based on a narrow interpretation of the bail provision as done in *Zahoor Ahmad Shah Watali*. Stan Swamy was another victim of this provision and its fallacious reading.

The top court has now altered this terrible legal landscape. For doing so, it also relied on a later three-judge bench decision in *Union of India v. K.A. Najeeb* (2021).[3] In *K.A. Najeeb*, the larger bench said that even the stringent provisions under Section 43D(5) do not curtail the power of the constitutional court to grant bail on the ground of violation of fundamental rights.

The text of draconian laws sometimes poses an immense challenge to the courts by limiting the space for judicial discretion and adjudication. This is all the more evident in the context of bail. The courts usually adopt two mutually contradictory methods in dealing with such tough provisions. One is to read and apply the provision literally and mechanically, which has the effect of curtailing individual freedom as intended by the makers of the law. In contrast to this approach, there could be a constitutional reading of the statute that perceives the issues from a human rights angle and tries to mitigate the rigour of the vicious content of the law. The former approach is reflected in *Zahoor Ahmad Shah Watali* and the latter in *Thwaha Fasal*. In *Thwaha Fasal*, the court has asserted the primacy of the judicial process over the text of the enactment, by way of an interpretative exercise.

---

[2] (2019) 5 SCC 1.
[3] (2021) 3 SCC 713.

Delhi Riots Case

On 15 June 2021, the Delhi High Court granted bail to student activists Natasha Narwal, Devangana Kalita and Asif Iqbal Tanha who were charged under the UAPA for alleged links with the Delhi riots. Responding to an appeal by the Delhi police, unfortunately, the Supreme Court said that the well-reasoned judgment of the High Court shall not be treated as a precedent.

The *Thwaha Fasal* judgment, by implication, has legitimized the methodology of the Delhi High Court verdict that ventured to examine the content of the charge instead of accepting the prosecution's story. It is such judicial radicalism that builds an emancipatory legal tool. The judgment should be invoked to release other political prisoners in the country who have been denied bail either due to the harshness of the law or due to follies in understanding the law, or both. Will that happen?

The Hindu, 8 November 2021, https://www.thehindu.com/opinion/lead/a-new-jurisprudence-for-political-prisoners/article37372642.ece.

ON POLITICS

25. Minister as Party Chief

This article was originally written when Amit Shah was retained as the president of the BJP even after occupying the position in the government as Home Minister. J.P. Nadda was initially chosen only as the working president of the party. He became president of the party on 20 January 2020. Thus the country had the same person as the Home Minister and the chief of the party that led the government for some time.

JAGAT PRAKASH NADDA's elevation as the working president of the Bharatiya Janata Party (BJP) pointed to Amit Shah's continuation as the party president. The Home Minister of the country also being the president of the ruling party posed serious questions of constitutional propriety as it could involve conflict of interest, in the larger sense of the phrase.

Time magazine journalist Olivia B. Waxman recently wrote that 'questions of profit in politics raised by the Trump administration are older than you may think'.[1] The linkage between the then US President and his family business had been in the media gaze for quite some time on the ground of conflict of interest. The idea is rooted in profiteering and business interest.

According to Articles 102(1) and 191(1) of our Constitution, a legislator is precluded from holding an office of profit under the government. But to put an end to the ethical dilemma of persons at the helm of affairs and to ensure the sanctity of the decision-making process, the concept of conflict of interest should transcend the commercial sense and should be taken as including political interest as well. The probity of governance requires stricter yardsticks. To quote M.J. Mafunisa, 'a primary reason for concern about conflicts of interest is that they reduce public trust and confidence in the integrity and impartiality of the public functionaries'.[2]

Article 74 of the Constitution speaks about a 'Council of Ministers' at the centre to 'aid and advise' the President. The President appoints a minister on the advice of the Prime Minister as per Article 75. It further implies that the minister should become a member of either House of Parliament within

---

[1] Olivia B. Waxman 'Questions of Profit in Politics Raised by Trump Administration are Older Than You May Think', 10 March 2017, https://time.com/4669729/conflict-of-interest-history/, accessed 9 January 2022.

[2] M.J. Mafunisa, 'Conflict of Interest: Ethical Dilemma in Politics and Administration', *South African Journal of Labour Relations*, vol. 27, no. 2, 2003.

at least six months of assuming office. This provision does not expressly bar the minister from acting as an office-bearer of a recognized political party. But it says that 'before a minister enters upon his office, the President shall administer to him the oaths of office and of secrecy according to the forms set out for the purpose in the Third Schedule'.

The content of the oath or affirmation under the Third Schedule is more important than its form. It requires the minister of the Union to 'bear true faith and allegiance to the Constitution of India as by law established'. The minister also needs to affirm that he/she 'will faithfully and conscientiously discharge [the] duties as a minister for the Union'. More significantly, the oath should be an open declaration that the minister 'will do right by all manner of people in accordance with the Constitution and the law, without fear or favour, affection or ill-will'.

Amit Shah took this oath and functioned as the country's Home Minister. But his continuation as president of the BJP, even if for a short time, clearly negated the intent and content of the oath. There is an implied prohibition under Article 75 of the Constitution against a minister heading his political party. The office of the party president presupposed the existence of political interest for Shah.

The BJP being the richest political party, can have various economic interests as well. Administration of the 'affairs of the Union' is to be done by the Council of Ministers, who should be 'collectively responsible' to the House of the people as per Articles 75 and 78 of the Constitution. This principle should equally apply to the state cabinets as well, since the scheme of Articles 164 and 167 dealing with the subject is more or less identical.

The double role assumed by Shah necessarily leads to conflict of interest. The violence in West Bengal in 2019 was an illustrative case. As the Union Home Minister, Shah was expected to take a neutral and judicious position in the matter, and ensure that the erring BJP leaders and workers in the state be made to face the due process of law. The same was expected of Chief Minister Mamata Banerjee as regards the miscreants belonging to her party.

Under the Seventh Schedule of the Constitution, though public order and the police come under the State List, criminal law and procedure are in the Concurrent List. In other words, law enforcement falls within the domain of the state government as well as the central government, in the manner provided by the Constitution. Curiously, in West Bengal, the Home Minister at the centre and the state's Chief Minister were the official heads of the rival political parties who accused each other of violence in the state.

Constitutional morality has to be the ideology of governance, both at the centre and in the states. Dual positions cannot meddle with the administration 'in accordance with the Constitution and the law'. At a time when political parties function like corporate entities, the economic interests of the parties or those who run the parties also cannot be ruled out. That, too, can run counter to the notion of fairness expected from the public offices. The argument that there are precedents of dual position in other political parties does not justify the inherent irony.

British economist and Margaret Thatcher's aide Tim Lankester once remarked: 'Societies need to guard against not just the actuality of conflict of interest intruding into official decision-making but also the perception that it may be doing so.'[3] Only when political corruption is properly conceived as a phenomenon not limited to financial transactions, will we understand the issue in the correct perspective. In India, conflict of interest in high offices can lead to clear instances of abuse of power and political arbitrariness.

Deccan Herald, 25 June 2019, https://www.deccanherald.com/opinion/main-article/minister-as-party-chief-742547.html

---

[3] Tim Lankester, 'Conflict of Interest: A Historical and Comparative Perspective', 5th Regional Seminar: Conflict of Interest: A Fundamental Anticorruption Concept, Asian Development Bank (ABD) and Organization for Economic Co-operation and Development (OECD), 2007.

26. Towards a Constitution Culture

This piece, written immediately after the Modi-2 regime came to power, raises scepticism about the political dispensation rooted in right-wing ideology and divisive politics. Unfortunately, today, the concerns expressed here have proved predictive.

PRIME MINISTER Narendra Modi bowed before a copy of the Constitution in Parliament after his party's victory in the Lok Sabha elections in 2019. The Indian National Congress leader Rahul Gandhi tweeted that his party MPs would strive 'to protect [the] Constitution and institutions'. It is now time to reflect on that socio-political document.

John Marshall, who was Chief Justice of the United States from 1801 to 1835, famously said that the constitution of a country is one 'framed for ages to come' and 'designed to approach immortality as near as human institutions can approach'. India's Constituent Assembly debates were fecund with imaginative deliberations. Apart from the mastermind Dr Ambedkar, the discourse included, among others, the optimist Nehru arguing for fundamental rights, Sardar Patel talking about the limits to freedom, Rajagopalachari pleading for Gandhian Swaraj and K.M. Munshi emphasizing personal liberty.

No constitution can protect itself. But it can engage and perpetuate a political culture necessary for its own preservation. In the words of the constitutional law scholar Mark Tushnet, 'It's politics, not "the Constitution", that is the ultimate – and sometimes the proximate – source for whatever protection we have for our fundamental rights.'[1]

The ruling coalition and the opposition have a political obligation to the country's fundamental law. But we need to travel beyond the rhetoric. The prime minister's gesture and Rahul Gandhi's tweet pose more questions than they answer.

The Constitution of India is also a cultural document. Unlike a religious text, it is intended for non-believers as well, as the great human rights lawyer K.G. Kannabiran once remarked. Building up a constitutional culture is not, however, an easy task. Dr Ambedkar warned that 'democracy in India is only

---

[1] Mark Tushnet, *Why the Constitution Matters*, Delhi: Universal Law Publishing Co., 2011, p. 1.

a top dressing'[2] and that the Indian society is 'essentially undemocratic'.[3] He reminded us about the great Indian 'contradiction' of how even while having political equality, the country struggles with social and economic inequality.[4]

Article 21 of the Constitution promises a dignified life, and Article 14 deals with equality. As the Nobel laureate Amartya Sen said, 'Poverty is not just a lack of money; it is not having the capability to realize one's full potential as a human being.'[5] Jurist Ronald Dworkin was quoted by journalist Stuart Jeffries in *The Guardian* as saying: 'I'm talking about dignity. It's a term overused by politicians, but any moral theory worth its salt needs to proceed from it.'[6] Dworkin's remarks indicate the true spirit of 'constitutional morality', a phrase India's top court has repeatedly invoked in different cases in recent times. We need to expand the idea of constitutional morality to address the fundamental issues of the country like poverty, illiteracy, unemployment and environmental degradation.

Jean Drèze says that 'the dismal living conditions of the Indian poor call for immediate intervention' and 'not a passive wait for economic growth to raise their per capita incomes'.[7] This would mean that poverty needs to be addressed as a severe threat to the country's Constitution that bears a socialist preamble offering 'justice – social, economic and political'. Good governance that focuses on improving people's living conditions alone would do justice to the intent and content of the basic law.

Dr Ambedkar envisaged a plan for 'State socialism by the law of the Constitution'. While proposing this idea, he rejected the possible criticism that the idea transcends 'the usual type of fundamental rights'. He indicated that the very purpose of enacting fundamental rights is to protect liberty and to evolve a fair economic structure.

Part IV of the Constitution, by way of the Directive Principles of State Policy, reflects the aspirations of the nation. Article 38 speaks about a just social order and people's welfare. Equal justice based on equal opportunity is the dream emanating from Article 39A. Article 41 mandates the state to ensure the citizen's right to work and education. This is followed by Article 42

---

[2] Constituent Assembly Debates, 4 November 1948.

[3] Ibid.

[4] Constituent Assembly Debates, 25 November 1949.

[5] Amartya Sen, @AmartyaSen_Econ, https://twitter.com/amartyasen_econ/status/70 3048545746751492?lang=en, 26 February 2016.

[6] Stuart Jeffries and Ronald Dworkin, 'We Have a Responsibility to Live Well', *The Guardian*, 31 March 2011.

[7] Jean Drèze, *Sense and Solidarity*, Ranikhet: Permanent Black, 2018, p. 57.

that calls for just and humane conditions of work, and Article 43 that pleads for a decent living wage. Themes under this part, ranging from agriculture to environmental protection, are all different facets of India's constitutional yearning. Dr Ambedkar wanted these principles to be 'the basis of all executive and legislative actions', and thus of governance. We will elaborate on these ideas in the concluding chapter.

It needs an imaginative project to connect the citizen with the affairs of governance. The term inclusive development is multifaceted. In a country of diversity where federalism and secularism are not just legal requirements but historical necessities, the political executive should guard against any kind of alienation, based on religion, territory or language. National integration must be rooted in the basic philosophy of socio-economic equality.

Political eloquence does not erase poverty or unemployment. It needs a constitutional praxis. Therefore, despite the gratifying gestures of the prime minister and the Congress leader, the citizens need to be sceptical, critical and also argumentative. The new regime needs to follow what the former US Supreme Court justice Robert Jackson said: 'It is not the function of our Government to keep the citizen from falling into error; it is the function of the citizen to keep the Government from falling into error.'[8]

The New Indian Express, 12 June 2019, https://www.newindianexpress.com/opinions/2019/jun/12/towards-a-constitution-culture-1989142.html

---

[8] *American Communications Assn, CIO et al. v. Douds,* Regional Director of the National Labour Relations Board 339 US 382, 1950, pp. 442–43.

27. When Hate is Also an Ideology

This updated article on hate speech was earlier written in the context of the Supreme Court's intervention in the Sudarshan TV case. A programme aired by the TV channel allegedly indicated that Muslims, with the help of foreign aid, have 'infiltrated' the civil services in India. The menace of spreading hatred in the guise of free speech needs to be tackled not only with legal tools, but also with pedagogical and political devices.

THE SUPREME COURT, on 15 September 2020, in an unprecedented move, interdicted Sudarshan television channel from telecasting a programme called 'Bindas Bol – UPSC Jihad'.[1] Many felt that the telecast was targeted against a particular religious community. A bench led by Justice Chandrachud was dealing with the legal and constitutional aspects of 'hate speech' in the media. The task before the court is to draw the subtle yet important distinction between free speech and hate speech.

British parliamentarian Bhikhu Parekh has said that '[hate speech] lowers the tone of public debate, coarsens the society's moral sensibility and weakens the culture of mutual respect'.[2] He explained that it 'violates the dignity of the target group by stigmatizing them, denying their capacity to live as responsible members of the society'. The Indian Supreme Court cautioned about the vices of hate speech in the cases *Babu Rao Patel v. State of Delhi* (1980)[3] and the *Pravasi Bhalai Sangathan v. Union of India* (2014).[4]

---

[1] *Firoz Iqbal Khan v. Union of India and Others* (2020), Writ Petition (Civil) No. 956/2020.

[2] Bhikhu Parekh, 'Limits of Free Speech', *Philosophia*, 45, 2017, pp. 931–35.

[3] (1980) 2 SCC 402. In this case, the appellant Babu Rao Patel, the editor, publisher and printer of a magazine, depicted the Muslim community as one with a 'racial tradition of rape, loot, violence and murder', and tried to justify it as a political thesis and historical truth. The Supreme Court rejected the contention and affirmed the conviction of the appellant for offences under Section 153A of the Indian Penal Code (Promoting enmity between different groups on the ground of religion, etc.).

[4] (2014) 11 SCC 477. In this public interest litigation, the petitioner organization prayed for action against hate speech by people's representatives and political/religious leaders. The Supreme Court disposed of the case with certain vital observations about the menace of hate speech, and underlying the role of law enforcement agencies and institutions like the Election Commission and the National Human Rights Commission in the matter.

Statutes against hate speech are not uncommon in liberal democracies. Section 14 of the Saskatchewan Human Rights Code in Canada prohibits publications that instigate hatred. India does not have a separate law on hate speech, although one can trace facets of it in different enactments including the Indian Penal Code (IPC). Rule 6 of the Cable Television Network Rules, 1994, prohibits programmes that offend 'good taste or decency', or contain matters 'contemptuous of religious groups' or promoting 'communal attitudes'.

There are other variants of hate speech enumerated in the Rule, though the phrase is not used. Section 5 of the Cable Television Networks (Regulation) Act speaks about programme code, which if violated can invite punishment as provided under Section 16 of the Act. Hate is more than an emotion or state of mind. It is an ideology. It is not limited to a few television shows or newspaper pieces. It is a contagious virus in the polity. It is antithetical to the spirit of the Constitution.

The Constituent Assembly debates have been published by the Lok Sabha Secretariat in huge volumes, in a commendable venture. In these debates, along with enormous erudition and expertise of the members, one finds a great deal of mutual tolerance and understanding. The members respected one another with a great sense of deliberative ethics. They built up an edifice for the nation through conversation. The Constitution, in a way, is this conversation crystallized.

No wonder, therefore, that we have a preamble in the fundamental law that talks not only about justice, liberty and equality, but also about fraternity. The preamble negates hate as an ideology and puts forward its own design for the nation in the making. The assertions of the nation resounded in Part III of the Constitution, dealing with fundamental rights. Part IV sets out the Directive Principles, which are the people's aspirations, as I have earlier noted.

These principles reflect the nation's dreams, ranging from gender equality to the community's control over resources. Article 51A(e) in Part IV A, which was incorporated later, talks about the duty to promote harmony and the spirit of 'common brotherhood' across 'religious, linguistic and regional or sectional diversities'. Article 51A(h) stresses on 'scientific temper and humanism'. Rhetoric on fraternity does not ensure its practice. The problem, however, is that we lose even the rhetoric. When fraternity is lost not merely in newsrooms but even in the legal and political landscape, the Constitution is betrayed.

The statutes based on hate do not pass constitutional muster even at a philosophical level. There is a line of thought that hate speech regulations are bad since such speech does not cause harm. It is however more plausible to think that hate speech does cause harm, as argued by Jeremy Waldron and others.

The state cannot punish the citizens for their individual choices, unless those harm the society. Laws cannot rest on imaginary postulates for punishing the citizen. There is enough empirical data from Uttar Pradesh to reveal the draconian character of the law on 'love jihad'. Victims are the best judges of the law. Many innocent people have demonstrated the inherent danger of such laws. The provisions are harsh and divisive.

The laws reflect the state's encroachment into forbidden zones of citizen's privacy. They interfere with the fundamental human instinct for intimacy and relationships. But these legislations do not emerge spontaneously; they happen in an enabling political climate. Hate laws that happened in certain states may not happen everywhere, at least for the time being. Law is politics with a legal terminology. Politics of hate cannot understand the quintessential relation between the nation, its people and the Constitution. On the other hand, it can transform to blatant incitement to violence, as happened in the Haridwar conclave in December 2021 which appealed for genocide of Muslims.

Instances of political murder or vigilantism in the country could be the manifestation of the detestation to which a section of the media also contributed. Physical and cyber threats against citizens for what they are or what they believe in have their origin in the political factories that manufacture and distribute hate. While conventional democracy rests on majoritarianism, constitutional democracy respects the minorities. Politics that does not honour the smaller lot cannot honour the citizens. To quote writer Ayn Rand, 'The smallest minority on earth is the individual.'

This is why a state with majoritarian impulses motivated by the doctrine of abhorrence hooks individuals by invoking its apparatus, ranging from police to prison. A stringent state can annihilate the individual's claim to dignity in the most heinous way. But India can no longer afford a gruesome state. We need to reread the country's Constitution as a condition for survival. The Constitution may not be eternal, but its values are.

The New Indian Express, 2 January 2021, https://www.newindianexpress.com/opinions/2021/jan/02/when-hateis-also-anideology-2244341.html.

28. Democracy, Dissent and the Courts

Written in the context of the movement against Citizenship Amendment Act, 2019 this article underlines the need for peaceful agitations as a means to resist the state's anti-people stand. It is relevant to revisit the ideas after the repeal of the farm laws.

THE ORDER ISSUED by the division bench of the Madras High Court on 22 December 2019 in a special Sunday night sitting[1] is a constitutional reminder to all of us. The bench of Justices S. Vaidyanathan and P.T. Asha refused to stay the rally against the Citizenship (Amendment) Act, 2019 (CAA) by the opposition parties, and permitted it but with stringent conditions so as to ensure that the protest is peaceful.

Freedom is non-negotiable. The protest against the CAA and the proposed National Register of Citizens (NRC) had a formidable logic behind it. It was the Union Home Minister who had earlier reiterated that the statute was inseparable from the scheme for an NRC. As such, one could legitimately think that the two-in-one package has a divisive and devastating agenda. Diversity in itself is a democratic virtue and the country's Constitution offers a secular future for its citizens.

True, Parliament has passed the law. The top court may validate or invalidate the statute. But a formal legislative or judicial process cannot and need not stall the citizen's right to protest. Peaceful protest based on dissent is democracy's first principle.

Violence in any form and from any side is to be condemned. In the anti-CAA protests, on several occasions the state was on the wrong side, and on other occasions, the protesters. Section 144 of the Criminal Procedure Code (CrPC) was invoked *en masse* in several states even though the protesters were violent only on a few occasions. Maintenance of public order is one thing; suppression of public protest is quite another. Section 144 provides for regulatory power, which is not akin to military power. The top court said in the Ramlila Maidan case (2012)[2] that 'minimum force' to avert a 'real' threat alone is justified.

---

[1] *Varaaki v. The Chief Secretary and Ors.*, writ petition nol. 35712/2019.

[2] (2012) 5 SCC 1. An anti-corruption rally was organized at Ramlila Maidan on 27 February 2011. Persons like Baba Ramdev were present at the venue. When permission to hold the camp was withdrawn, during the night hours, personnel belonging to Delhi Police, Rapid Action Force and Central Reserve Police Force

Earlier, a seven-judge bench of the Supreme Court, in *Madhu Limaye v. Sub Divisional Magistrate* (1970),[3] endorsed the constitutional validity of Section 144 of the CrPC, by reiterating the principle in an earlier decision, *Babulal Parate v. State of Maharashtra* (1961).[4] In *Madhu Limaye*, the court also underlined the 'safeguards' available for the dissidents. It held that 'the gist of action under Section 144 is the urgency of the situation'. To justify the invocation of Section 144, 'the emergency must be sudden and the consequences sufficiently grave'. Therefore, it follows that an unreasonable general order made in advance with a view to prevent public protest would be vulnerable to legal challenge. Likewise, police killings also required detailed investigation and magisterial enquiry based on the guidelines of the top court in *PUCL v. State of Maharashtra* (2014).[5] It is doubtful whether there was compliance of the People's Union for Civil Liberties (PUCL) directives in the incidents of police firing against some of the anti-CAA protesters.

In *Puttaswamy v. Union of India* (2017),[6] the top court said that dignity and privacy are facets of right to life under Article 21 of the Constitution. Relying heavily on the principles in *Puttaswamy*, Justice P.V. Asha of the Kerala High Court held that the action of curtailing the access to information through the internet amounts to unreasonable restriction on the freedom of the citizens.[7] The principle of law laid down in *Puttaswamy* and the emphasis on individual autonomy given in that verdict is the law of the land. Viewed so, the state's repeated actions of curtailing the internet in order to suppress the people's movement against CAA also does not pass constitutional muster.

The police have to be vigilant to preserve public property and to proceed against the offenders, as held by the apex court (in *Re: Destruction of Public*

---

reached the venue and forcefully tried to evict the protesters. In the matter, the Supreme Court found fault with the executive action.

[3] (1970) 3 SCC 746.

[4] AIR 1961 SC 884.

[5] (2014) 10 SCC 635. About 99 alleged encounters between Mumbai Police and the alleged criminals caused the death of 135 persons in a period of about two years (1995–97). The petitioner organization raised the issue of fake encounters.

[6] (2017) 10 SCC 1, Justice Puttaswamy (Retd.) challenged the mandatory imposition of the Aadhaar scheme as violative of the right to privacy and thereby ignoring the dignity of citizens.

[7] Judgment dated 19 September 2019 in Writ Petition (Civil) No. 19716/2019. The prohibition against the use of mobile phones and laptops in a college hostel was held to be unreasonable.

& Private Properties, 2009).[8] No doubt, when a mob turns violent, the police has the duty to deal with the situation, even by invoking force. But that does not mean unbridled power. A Karnataka minister mentioned the Godhra episode (2002, where Hindu pilgrims were killed in a train fire, which in turn triggered communal riots) in his response to the protests. A minister at the centre also publicly said that offenders will be 'shot at sight'. It is a sad irony that these statements came at a time when a constitution bench of the apex court in *Kaushal Kishore v. The State of Uttar Pradesh*[9] was considering the question relating to such provocative and disparaging utterances by ministers and others holding constitutional posts.

The right to hold peaceful demonstrations and public meetings is protected by Article 19(1)(a), (b) and (c) of the Constitution. The idea of civil disobedience, advanced by Henry David Thoreau and practised and propagated by Mahatma Gandhi and Martin Luther King, Jr., mandates that even disobedience has to be civil and not criminal, which means that protests should be peaceful and non-violent. The top court in *Nawabkhan Abbaskhan v. State of Gujarat* (1974)[10] quoted justice Benjamin Curtis, who talked about the 'patriotic duty of a citizen to raise a question whether a law is within the Constitution of the country'. The top court even referred to a clause in a German state Constitution, to say that 'it is the right and duty of every man to resist unconstitutionally exercised public power'.

It is only peaceful protest and open criticism that make democracy genuine and vibrant. In the words of the former American Judge Robert H. Jackson, 'Those who begin coercive elimination of dissent soon find themselves exterminating dissenters. Compulsory unification of opinion achieves only the unanimity of the graveyard.'[11]

The New Indian Express, 28 December 2019, https://www.newindianexpress.com/opinions/2019/dec/28/democracy-dissent-and-the-courts-2081872.html.

---

[8] (2009) 5 SCC 212. The Supreme Court, in this case, constituted two committees to examine the impact of the massive destruction of properties during agitations, *hartals*, etc. The court said that 'the suggestions (of the Committee) are extremely important and they constitute sufficient guidelines which need to be adopted'.

[9] WP(C) 113/2016. In this case, the Supreme Court is considering the issue of restrictions on the utterance of public functionaries on public platforms. The case is pending, as on 28 November 2021.

[10] (1974) 2 SCC 121.

[11] *West Virginia State Board of Education ET AL v. Barnette ET AL* 319 U.S. 624 (1943).

29. Tyranny of the Majority

This article is an attempt to trace the clear shift in legislative process in recent India. The change is marked by glaring unconstitutionality or lack of deliberation or a political agenda. This trend has accelerated incrementally (see chapter 1, 'When Laws Subvert the Constitution'). Sadly, even at the end of 2021, the apex court had not decided on the validity of many of the laws referred to in this article.

'INQUIRIES INTO CONGRESSIONAL motives or purposes are a hazardous matter', said Chief Justice Warren in *US v. O'Brien* (1968).[1] The statement represents the conventional reluctance of the constitutional court, as the umpire of democracy, to assess the motivation of the legislature in deciding the validity of an enactment. According to this line of thinking, the Constitution cannot be used as 'an instrument for punishing the evil thoughts of members of the political branches' as John Hart Ely, who was Associate Professor of Law at Yale University, put it.[2] The tyranny of the majority was manifest in the intent and content of almost all recent legislative attempts in the Indian Parliament. The 'evil thoughts' were writ large in criminalizing a judicially invalidated civil wrong, which we noted in chapter 2; in 'centralizing' the Right to Information Act; and in equipping the centre with the power to label anyone a terrorist.

Therefore, the Indian courts may have to deviate from the habit of attributing good faith to the legislations when called upon to decide the constitutional validity of recent laws made, unmade or remade by the Parliament. The courts will have to deal with unconstitutional motivations in legislations in the process of judicial review.

Any legislation is bound to reflect a political ideology. A comparison of some of the recent legislative ventures with the laws made by Parliament earlier would demonstrate a clear shift from the process of democratic law-making to populist and centralizing legislations.

The Indian Parliament has a legacy of bringing in statutes dealing with the right to free and compulsory education (2009), the right to food security

---

[1] 391 US 367 (1968).
[2] John Hart Ely, 'Legislative and Administrative Motivation in Constitutional Law', *The Yale Law Journal*, vol. 79, no. 7, June 1970, p. 1216.

(2013), etc.[3] The incorporation of the word 'socialism' in the preamble to the Constitution in 1977 had its statutory resonances, though belatedly. Now, one finds a tragic fall in the quality of legislative content, thanks to the advent of the far right at the helm of political bodies.

Not everything was fine, however, with earlier regimes. A draconian legislation is the manifestation of an aggrandizing state. Such legislations were passed during the Emergency (1975–77) and even thereafter. The Congress party also owes an apology to the country for their legislative misadventures and misdeeds. Laws like the Terrorist and Disruptive Activities (Prevention) Act (TADA) and Prevention of Terrorism Act (POTA) victimized thousands of activists, journalists, lawyers and political leaders across the country. Many of them were ultimately found to be innocent by the competent courts. It is curious that the Bharatiya Janata Party, which initially claimed to be the 'party with a difference', has followed suit and placed itself on the wrong side of history.

The Political and Constitutional Reforms Committee of the House of Commons in the UK published a report titled 'Ensuring standards in the quality of legislations' (2013–2014), which said that 'the primary reason for poor-quality legislation was political'.[4] It quoted British MP Nick Raynsford, who remarked that political pressure reduces the law-making exercise to an 'evidence of action' or 'test of a government's political standing'. In the process, the long-term consequences of the law on the public at large are widely ignored. The report underlines the significance of the Legislative Standards Committee in ensuring good-quality laws, and pleads for pre- and post-legislative scrutiny.

Like the 103rd Constitutional Amendment Act, which contemplated economic reservation with a 10 per cent quota exclusively for the forward communities, the recent legislations in India on triple talaq and Right to Information needed pre-legislative deliberation and constitutional scrutiny.[5]

When the validity of triple talaq itself was the subject matter of the

---

[3] There were more such welfare enactments during the United Progressive Alliance (UPA) regime (2004–14). See chapter 1.

[4] Political and Constitutional Reform Committee, 'Ensuring standards in the quality of legislation', *First Report of Session 2013–14, Volume I*, House of Commons, London, United Kingdom, 20 May 2013.

[5] By way of the 2019 amendment to the Right to Information Act, 2005, terms of service, salary and allowances were altered as matters 'to be prescribed by the Central Government'. Clearly, this amendment would enhance the control of the government over the Information Commissioners, curtailing the latter's independence.

Supreme Court judgment in *Shayara Bano* (2017), its criminalization, which we examined in chapter 2, required a serious deliberation. The dilution and annihilation of the citizen's right to know by way of the 2019 amendment needed examination in the light of the Supreme Court's verdicts on Right to Information, mainly in the *Indira Nehru Gandhi v. Raj Narain* (1975)[6] and *People's Union for Civil Liberties [PUCL] v. Union of India* (2003)[7] cases.

These legislations, like the one on 10 per cent quota for the economically backward, are also likely to be scanned by the top court. The quality of the enactments, which could not get the benefit of examination by parliamentary committees, may be exposed in adjudicative process. Ultimately, it is the constitutional test that will possibly rescue the country from reckless legislations with draconian content.

The letter by seventeen opposition parties to the Rajya Sabha chairman says that in the 14th Lok Sabha, 60 per cent of the bills were referred to parliamentary committees and in the 15th Lok Sabha, 71 per cent of them were referred.[8] But under the first Modi government, only 26 per cent of the bills were sent for scrutiny; and the current Lok Sabha has passed 14 bills without sending any of them to the parliamentary committees.

The dependence of the legislators on expert opinions and views reflected in public discourse is a principle that the present dispensation has chosen to ignore. As James Madison famously pointed out, accumulation of legislative power in the elected majority could also lead to negation of democracy.

Deccan Herald, 8 August 2019, https://www.deccanherald.com/opinion/in-perspective/tyranny-of-majority-752836.html.

---

[6] (1975) 2 SCC 159.

[7] (2003) 4 SCC 399. Both these cases underline the significance of informational rights of the citizenry in the Indian constitutional context. The spirit of the verdict is reflected in the Right to Information Act, 2005 as it was originally designed.

[8] '17 Opposition Parties Write to Venkaiah Naidu over Passage of Bills Without Any Scrutiny', *The Hindu*, 26 July 2019, available at https://www.thehindu.com/news/national/17-opposition-parties-write-to-venkaiah-naidu-over-passage-of-bills-without-any-scrutiny/article28721328.ece, accessed 2 December 2021.

30. Rule of Law during Elections

The West Bengal Assembly election in 2021 was preceded by frequent raids by central agencies on the premises of opposition leaders in the state. This was neither the first nor the last of its kind. The episodes indicate a new normal in the realm of power.

INDEPENDENCE OF THE investigating agencies has been a case of judicial romanticism in India. In *Prakash Singh v. Union of India* (2006),[1] the Supreme Court said that such apparatus should 'secure professional independence'. and 'function truly and efficiently as an impartial agent of the law of the land'. Though the Court was dealing with the police system in the country in general, the jurisprudence reflected in the judgment should apply to the agencies under the centre as well. In *Vineet Narain and Ors v. Union of India and Anr.* (1997),[2] popularly known as the Hawala case, the Supreme Court underlined the need for functional autonomy for the Central Bureau of Investigation (CBI). But in 2013, the same court had to say that the CBI acted like a 'caged parrot speaking in its master's voice'. These remarks came while it was considering the coal allocation case. The criticism was that those who were closer to the power centres enjoyed impunity in corruption cases. At present, the primary role of the agency seems to be to subserve the political interest of its master. Thus, the CBI appears to be an unkind weapon in the hands of the state. It is a device to suppress criticism and oppress the opponents.

The Enforcement Directorate (ED) is an agency empowered to enforce the Foreign Exchange Management Act (FEMA), 1999 and the Prevention of Money Laundering Act (PMLA), 2002. The agency is also given the task of

---

[1] (2006) 8 SCC 1. This writ petition initiated by Prakash Singh, a former officer of the Indian Police Service, has paved way for judicial prescriptions for reforms in the police system in the country. But many of the directions of the Supreme Court are yet to be implemented on the ground level.

[2] (1998) 1 SCC 226. On 25 March 1991, an alleged terrorist arrested from Delhi was questioned. Based on information so received, raids were conducted in which, apart from currency notes, two diaries and two notebooks were seized containing the names of political and bureaucratic bigwigs. When the investigation stagnated thereafter, due to alleged political and other influences, a public interest litigation (PIL) was filed by journalist Vineet Narain before the Hon'ble Supreme Court that led to this verdict.

dealing with cases under certain other laws like Fugitive Economic Offenders Act, 2018. Clearly the agency has an important duty to maintain economic security.

The National Investigation Agency (NIA) is the major anti-terrorist task force in India. Paradoxically, in recent times, not only political opponents but even independent intellectuals, activists and journalists have been targeted by the agency, invoking draconian laws like the Unlawful Activities Prevention Act (UAPA).

According to the Seventh Schedule of the Constitution, public order and the police fall under the State List, but criminal law and criminal procedure generally come under the Concurrent List. The centre enjoys supremacy over subjects falling under the Concurrent List, inasmuch as central laws on a given subject can prevail over state laws. As a result, the states are relatively helpless to resist the excesses of central agencies. The only way out at the state level is to avail a timely judicial intervention in the matter, which, however, seldom happens. Ideally, these agencies and other agencies like the Income Tax Department should act fairly, legally and in the service of the people at large.

The ED claims to aim to 'be fair and reasonable' in its investigations. It purportedly 'take decisions without fear or favour' and will 'act without malice, prejudice or bias and not allow the abuse of power'.[3] This, however, is contrary to the ground reality.

Laws can be dangerous if their invocation is not fair. The misuse of laws is often not merely a legal aberration but the result of conscious political decisions. When politics in its rudimentary form replaces governance and administration, laws, along with their instrumentalities, could very well turn into weapons to execute the agenda of those holding power.

But it is erroneous to think that misuse of the agencies only shows adherence to the immediate seats of power. It also reflects an ideology that disregards the institutions of governance – both constitutional and statutory. In the process, the centre shows scant regard to the tenets of the rule of law. Governance in India is now replaced by crummy politics. Under the new dispensation, merit or scientific temperament or legal expertise has no place. Votes alone matter, not even lives, as demonstrated in the 'dance of democracy' that occurred in the election to five Assemblies in 2021. The Election Commission also failed to act as a strong and impartial umpire of the system, though its duty under Article 324 of the Constitution is pivotal.

---

[3] Official website of the Enforcement Directorate, https://enforcementdirectorate. gov.in/corevalues.html?p1=12110181637252294572, accessed 18 November 2021.

A Muted Election Commission

Let us take the case of West Bengal. The raids conducted on the premises of opposition leaders were ostensibly political in nature.[4] The Election Commission (EC) was practically muted. This was followed by an unprecedented excess unleashed by the Central Industrial Security Force (CISF) in Bengal that resulted in the killing of four workers of the Trinamool Congress (TMC). It happened on 10 April 2021. The raids in Bengal were only a repetition of the theatrics that happened elsewhere – in Karnataka, Rajasthan and Tamil Nadu.

In another part of the country, the Kerala High Court, on 16 April 2021, quashed FIRs registered by Kerala Police against officers of the ED. The allegation was that the officers had fabricated evidence. According to the FIR, the ED coerced the accused in the sensational gold smuggling case to implicate Chief Minister Pinarayi Vijayan and a few other top officers in the state. Justice V.G. Arun quashed the FIR by relying on the conditions and prohibitions against such prosecution in the Criminal Procedure Code. But the very fact that there was a glaring conflict between the central agencies and the state police is antithetical to the idea of the rule of law in a federal set-up.

As the Supreme Court held in *Manoj Narula v. Union of India* (2014),[5] good governance is a constitutional imperative. But the centre has long forgotten the fundamentals of constitutional governance in its march towards a regime of far-right ideology blended with Hindutva objectives. The priorities are deplorable especially given the hard economic and health realities in the country.

Many of the basic features of the Constitution are interlinked. The absolutism and centrist approach of the present regime is a composite attack

---

[4] During March and April 2021, the central agencies carried out a series of incursions in the establishments of the TMC leaders in West Bengal. Mamata Banerjee alleged that the agencies have been 'brazenly and vindictively' used by the centre. 'In 'Election Season, the Raids are Back – Against Opposition Leaders', *The Hindustan Times*, 5 April 2021 https://www.hindustantimes.com/india-news/in-election-season-the-raids-are-back-against-opposition-leaders-101617609673969.html, accessed 9 November 2021.

[5] (2014) 9 SCC 1. A public interest petition by Manoj Narula challenged the appointment of political leaders who were accused of committing heinous crimes. Though concrete directions were not issued as the selection of ministers was the prerogative of the Prime Minister or the Chief Minister, the court advocated for avoiding persons with unclean track records. The court underlined the doctrine of constitutional trust to be followed while choosing a cabinet minister.

on all these features, which include rule of law, federalism, republicanism, institutional justice and fair elections.

The ultimate solution is to regain the values of the Constitution. It is much more than a design for governance. It is a viable safeguard against anarchy as well as autocracy. Therefore, we must realize that the Constitution of the country is also a means to politically educate ourselves and to demonstrate the resulting wisdom in the everyday public life. This idea is explained further in the last chapter.

Deccan Herald, 18 April 2021, https://www.deccanherald.com/specials/sunday-spotlight/rule-of-law-fails-politicsgains-975643.html.

31. The Anti-CAA Movement

Though many await the court's decision on the Citizenship Amendment Act (CAA) and the preparation of the National Register of Citizens (NRC), as we noted in chapter 28, the people's movement against such discriminatory legislative practices will always remain a relevant democratic tool. The anti-CAA movement needs to take lessons from the victorious struggle of the Indian farmers. The anti-CAA movement may not get public support as in the case of the farmers' struggle due to the communal colour attributed to it. This is all the more the reason to focus on the constitutional theme of the objection against the CAA and the NRC. This article, originally written prior to the farmers' agitation, reasserts the role of people's solidarity against formal majoritarianism in the legislature.

T HE POLITICAL ASPECT of the Citizenship Amendment Act is more significant than the legal aspect. Therefore, it is unsafe and even unwise to wait for what the Supreme Court may say on the subject and to dispense with peaceful protests during the interregnum. It is equally unwise for every serious political leader or civil rights activist, or even a citizen, for that matter, to move the court with a blind sense of optimism. There is nothing like an abstract constitutional issue, for every constitutional issue is essentially political. As the scholar Granville Austin remarked, 'Equipped with the basic qualifications, attitudes, and experience for creating and working a democratic constitution, Indians did not default their tryst with destiny.'[1] Professor Mark Tushnet rightly said: 'People disagree about what our fundamental rights are, and no one really believes that whatever the Supreme Court says those rights are is the last word.'[2]

Whether the Supreme Court has acted as the guardian of the Constitution during critical situations is a crucial question. When confronted with an aggrandizing state with a mighty executive and disquieting legislative majority, the top court has often, if not always, failed to rescue the citizenry. It refused to strike down undemocratic legislations like the Terrorist and Disruptive

---

[1] Granville Austin, *The Indian Constitution: Cornerstone of a Nation*, Delhi: Oxford University Press, 1999.

[2] Mark Tushnet, *Why the Constitution Matters*, Delhi: Universal Law Publishing Co., first Indian reprint, 2011.

Activities (Prevention) Act, 1987 (TADA) and the Prevention of Terrorism Act, 2002 (POTA). Rampant misuse of the Unlawful Activities (Prevention) Act, 1967 (UAPA) remains judicially unchecked. The Armed Forces (Special Powers) Act, 1958 (AFSPA) also was not interfered with despite its widespread misuse in North East India.[3] The most powerful Supreme Court in the world could not effectively prevent the detention of Kanhaiya Kumar,[4] Sudha Bharadwaj[5] or others for a long time. More significantly, it remained 'committed' to the power centres during the dark days of the Emergency in 1975–77.

Dark days are here again. When demonetization was met with a legal challenge,[6] the top court refused to stall the egregious folly, even though there were ostensible legal grounds to do that, like the absence of parliamentary sanction and statutory support for the decision. Thus the court allowed the resultant calamities to happen. The court had then referred the matters to a constitution bench.[7] Such a bench is yet to be constituted. It was not only for executive highhandedness but for judicial apathy as well that the country had to pay a hefty price. We have explored the court's passive attitude in such situations in the earlier chapters.

To put it bluntly, in the context of the CAA and the National Register of Citizens (NRC), litigation is not a democratic substitute for the praxis of peaceful agitation. No wonder that the TADA and the POTA were repealed by Parliament when the people of the country, and not the court, 'declared' them as 'unconstitutional'. It was an instance of peaceful democratic dissent correcting an arrogant and violent state. It marked the triumph of constitutionalism. The Constitution advances not invariably through the court; rather, it flourishes on the streets.

---

[3] All these enactments were promulgated under the guise of the government's fight against terrorism and insurgency in the country. However, on the ground, the laws revealed the instances of state terrorism. For a detailed discussion on AFSPA, see chapter 43.

[4] Kanhaiya Kumar was arrested for sloganeering on the Jawaharlal Nehru University campus in the year 2016 on an allegation of sedition.

[5] Sudha Bharadwaj, an accused in the Bhima Koregaon case, was in prison for more than three years until she was released on 9 December 2021 after being granted default bail by the Bombay High Court on 1 December 2021.

[6] *Vivek Narayan Sharma v. Union of India* (2016), (2017) 1 SCC 388. In the said case, the notification dated 8 November 2016 regarding demonetization of currency notes of Rs 500 and Rs 1,000 was challenged.

[7] Order dated 16 December 2016 in *Vivek Narayan Sharma*. See note 6 above.

The substitution of mass protests by litigation does not necessarily enrich democracy. In an interview, philosopher Charles Taylor was anxious about 'the best and brightest minds in America' being 'concerned exclusively with fighting out the major battles in Supreme Court decisions'.[8]

The politics of the CAA needs to be fixed in its historical context. It started with views on citizenship based on religion as infamously propounded by the Rashtriya Swayamsevak Sangh (RSS)'s second chief M.S. Golwalkar, in his book *Bunch of Thoughts* (first published 1966). It is inseparable from the National Population Register (NPR) and the NRC, and from the politics of state terrorism. It is again a significant political argument that the present move is also aimed at diverting the public dissatisfaction over the poor state of the Indian economy. This, too, is an aspect that the court cannot consider. Thus the politics of the CAA, in all senses, transcends the narrow compass of constitutional adjudication.

The legislature, too, has a duty to protect the citizen's freedoms. It needs to stick to the core values of the fundamental law. The present Article 19[9] (which was Article 13 in the draft of the Constitution) was a subject widely discussed while making the Constitution. The state can also restrict freedoms as per the Article. Therefore, even in the Constituent Assembly debates, an apprehension was raised whether the clause in the Constitution enabling the restriction of freedom is excessive. B.R. Ambedkar, K. Hanumanthaiya, Shibban Lal Saksena, T.T. Krishnamachari and Algu Rai Shastri, however, brushed aside the anxieties. Algu Rai Shastri said: '[The legislature] will impose only those restrictions which they consider proper. . . . No restriction will be imposed merely to destroy the liberties of the people.' It is this trust bestowed on the Parliament that stands betrayed by the majoritarian onslaught that paved the way to the CAA. In the post-CAA phase, Article 19 became *non est* in many parts of the nation.

Justice Krishna Iyer dealt with the question of 'lawlessness of law or order' by referring to the idea of civil disobedience (*Nawabkhan Abbaskhan v. State*

---

[8] Richard Kearney, *States of Mind: Dialogues with Contemporary Thinkers on the European Mind*, Manchester: Manchester University Press, 1995.

[9] Article 19(1): All citizens shall have the right: (a) to freedom of speech and expression; (b) to assemble peaceably and without arms; (c) to form associations or unions; (d) to move freely throughout the territory of India; (e) to reside and settle in any part of the territory of India; (g) to practise any profession, or to carry on any occupation, trade or business. Articles 19(2) to 19(6) deal with reasonable restrictions on these freedoms.

of Gujarat [1974]).[10] He quoted former US Supreme Court judge Benjamin Curtis to say that 'it may be and has been a high and patriotic duty of citizens to raise a question whether a law is within the Constitution of the country'.

India's contribution to modern jurisprudence is predominantly made by a lawyer-politician – M.K. Gandhi. It was the praxis of civil disobedience marked by peace and non-violence that underlined the need for people's oppositional radicalism in unjust political situations. Protest is not an easy task in a police state. Still, it remains a democratic imperative and a means of emancipation.

Deccan Herald, 20 February 2020, https://www.deccanherald.com/opinion/main-article/ anti-caa-movement-litigationnot-a-democratic-substitute-for-the-praxis-of-peaceful agitation-806633.*html*.

[10] (1974) 2 SCC 121.

32. Violence Has No Constitutional Endorsement

The Maoist insurgency in India is a serious threat to constitutionalism. Nevertheless, under the guise of counter-insurgency strategies, the state cannot resort to extra-constitutional devices. The fake encounters in Kerala are disturbing, A course correction is indispensable.

IN 1999, JUSTICE C.S. Rajan of the Kerala High Court directed the Central Bureau of Investigation (CBI) to investigate into an 'encounter killing' that occurred on 18 February 1970. Varghese, a Naxalite leader, was shot dead in Thirunelli forest in Kerala.

After a few decades, a police constable named Ramachandran Nair, out of an intense sense of remorse, revealed that it was he who shot Varghese, pursuant to orders from superior officers. He filed an affidavit to that effect before the High Court, and the court thereupon directed a fresh probe into the matter. It was not an encounter killing any more.

The case was investigated and a charge sheet was filed. The trial ended in conviction. Nair, who said that he did the act but not the offence, as he was only an instrument in the brutal event, died before the verdict. A superior police officer, Inspector General Lakshmana, who had retired, was punished and sent to prison in 2010, forty years after the incident.

One does not find many parallels for this episode. Public conscience as well as the conscience of Ramachandran Nair generated a unique sense of justice in Kerala's civil society, that in turn acted as an effective check on the state's police power. The state was constantly under people's trial, as an offshoot of Varghese's martyrdom.

The times have changed. Changes have occurred in legal landscape. Justice too has had its post-truth versions. The government's gesture, the public's perception and the media's approach on such issues are no longer the same. The state eventually regained its gruesome insensitivity as it began to misuse its revolvers quite frequently. S. Velmurugan, a suspected Maoist, was shot dead on 3 November 2020 by the 'Thunderbolt' force[1] in Kerala. This, according to the Kerala government, was again an 'encounter killing', though no constable was injured and no damage caused to the force. Velmurugan was

---

[1] Kerala Thunderbolts was formed as directed by the centre for counter-insurgency strategies in the state.

the eighth alleged Maoist to be shot dead in so-called encounters with the police after the Left government was elected in 2016.

Terrorism is antithetical to constitutionalism and Maoism is not an exception. Violence by itself is dangerous and deplorable. It has never been a genuine solution to any human problem in our long history. Political extremism based on violence cuts at the very root of peaceful coexistence. Maoism in India has been anti-social, preposterous and barbaric. Indian Maoists are indubitably on the wrong side of history.

The question, however, is whether violence by the state has legal sanction and constitutional legitimacy. The Maoists do not believe in the Constitution of the country. But remarkably, the Constitution also stands for those who do not honour it. The duty of a democratic government is to book the culprits and subject them to the due process of law. That would help in understanding the root causes of insurgency and eradicating it.

Unfortunately, Chief Minister Pinarayi Vijayan's position on the issue has been undemocratic and disappointing. He endorses almost every police action. He repeats what the police say. The Chief Minister had earlier justified the arrest and detention of two young students booked for alleged Maoist link. They were arrested in November 2019 and detained in prison for about a year, till they were released on bail by the special court in September. We have examined this case in detail in chapter 24. The special court found that in the case, *prima facie*, there was no act of violence or incitement to commit any offence. An ideological belief on its own does not constitute an offence. The Supreme Court had clarified this position in *Arup Bhuyan v. State of Assam* (2011)[2] when it said that mere sympathy with a banned organization without any kind of incitement to violence is not an offence. A non-violent and harmless belief evidently does not involve culpability, said the court.

The judgments in *Sri Indra Das v. State of Assam* (2011)[3] followed suit. The US decision in *Elfbrandt v. Russell* (1966),[4] where the court rejected the theory of 'guilt by [mere] association' was followed by the Indian Supreme Court. The Kerala High Court in *Shyam Balakrishnan v. State of Kerala* (2015)[5] and the Bombay High Court in *Jyoti Babasaheb Chorge v. State of Maharashtra* (2012)[6] agreed with this.

[2] (2011) 3 SCC 377.
[3] (2011) 3 SCC 380.
[4] 384 US 11 (1966).
[5] 2015 (2) KLT 927.
[6] 2012 SCC OnLine Bom 1460.

In their analysis of Maoist insurgency and counter-insurgency in India, Jonathan Kennedy and Sunil Purushotham concluded that the strategy of our regimes has 'pushed Maoist insurgency to the margins of Indian political life but has been unable to eliminate insurgent activity or address the fundamental grievances of adivasis'.[7]

The Maoist threat is a serious issue that calls for strategic solutions. The nation needs to handle it efficiently, yet lawfully. The threat is not peculiar to Kerala. Its gravity is severe in several other states. Still, every bullet in Kerala is a shock, since the state is ranked first in terms of good governance, followed by the other south Indian states of Tamil Nadu, Andhra Pradesh and Karnataka. Good governance is a constitutional aspiration, as explained by the top court in the *Manoj Narula* case (2014; see chapter 30). Clearly, fake encounters hit at the very idea of good governance. This is why Kerala matters. It matters for India and for all Indians.

The New Indian Express, 15 November 2020, https://www.newindianexpress.com/opinions/2020/nov/15/violence-has-no-constitutional-sanction-2223761.html.

[7] From the 'Abstract' of Jonathan Kennedy and Sunil Purushotham, 'Beyond Naxalbari: A Comparative Analysis of Maoist Insurgency and Counterinsurgency in Independent India', *Comparative Studies in Society and History*, vol. 54, no. 4, pp. 832–62, available at https://www.jstor.org/stable/23274553, accessed 11 December 2021.

33. Defection, Corruption and the Law

Political leaders shift their allegiance, very often, due to personal ambitions rather than ideological compulsions. This is a serious issue that impacts democracy's credentials. Turncoats enjoying peculiar privileges represent the new normal in Indian politics. Sadly, the legal system is incapable of handling it.

A SPECIAL FEATURE OF Indian politics is the ease with which turncoats often talk politics. Those who were spokespersons of a particular political party till yesterday will preach the exact opposite on a fine morning, speaking on behalf of a rival party. The public does not seem very uncomfortable with this shift, although it plainly insults their intelligence.

Perhaps these moments directly epitomize the ethical level of Indian politics. On the eve of the Assembly elections held during March and April 2021, there were a large number of defectors across the board. In states like West Bengal, the very contest is founded upon pre-election repudiations and tactical affiliations. Now that the elections are over and results announced, in the particular context of West Bengal, after Mamata Banerjee's victory, many who left the Trinamool Congress have come back to it, regretting the 'error in their initial judgment'.

Changing party lines is not a new phenomenon in India. In the early decades of Independence, there were many illustrative cases of political opportunism. B. Venkatesh Kumar, in an article in *Economic and Political Weekly*, writes:

> Between the fourth and fifth general elections in 1967 and 1972, from among the 4,000 odd members of the Lok Sabha and the Legislative Assemblies in the states and the Union Territories, there were nearly 2,000 cases of defection and counter-defection. By the end of March 1971, approximately 50% of the legislators had changed their party affiliations and several of them did it more than once – some of them as many as five times.[1]

We always had our '*aaya Rams*' and '*gaya Rams*'.[2] The original Constitution

---

[1] B. Venkatesh Kumar, 'Anti-Defection Law: Welcome Reforms', *Economic and Political Weekly*, vol. 38, no. 19, 10 May 2003.

[2] Gaya Lal, a Member of the Legislative Assembly in Haryana, won the elections in 1967 as an independent candidate. He thereafter joined the Indian National

did not foresee this trick of the trade, and the enormous amount of money and power play involved in it. Therefore, by way of the 52nd Amendment Act to the Constitution, the Tenth Schedule was incorporated in 1985. The object was to disqualify members of the legislature if they committed defection. This is popularly known as the anti-defection law.

But the law failed. Clause 2(1)(a) of the Tenth Schedule disqualifies a member of the legislature if he voluntarily gives up membership of his/her political party. Clause 2(1)(b) broadly indicates that breach of the directive given by the political party would invite disqualification of the member.

Mr Bumble, a character in *Oliver Twist* by Charles Dickens, famously suggested that the law could be an idiot on certain occasions. Mocking the Tenth Schedule, politicians could topple and form governments across states by institutionalizing defection. Resignation became the new methodology that defeated the text of the Tenth Schedule. In Karnataka[3] and Madhya Pradesh,[4] many members of the Assembly resigned, overturning elected governments and installing new regimes. And many of the defectors were successful in the polls that followed. People happily re-elected them under a new political label. Post-election coalitions in Karnataka and Maharashtra also certainly betrayed people's mandates.

It is a tragedy that defection is no longer seen as unethical. It is taken as an act of political cleverness that often bears brand names like 'Operation Lotus'. But if we are serious about the quality of democracy, it is time to rethink our jurisprudence on political defection. Clause 7 of the Tenth Schedule was struck down by the constitution bench of the Supreme Court in *Kihoto Hollohan v. Zachillu* (1992).[5] Clause 7, on the face of it, was unconstitutional,

---

Congress and then changed his party thrice, within just two weeks. On his arrival back in the Congress, it was announced by a Congress leader that 'Gaya Ram has now become Aaya Ram'. This episode created a new political jargon – *aaya Rams, gaya Rams* – to refer to frequent defections and counter-defections, turncoats, etc., among members of political parties. The incident also marked the egregious side of political defection in India in the 1960s and thereafter.

[3] T.A. Johnson and C.G. Manoj, 'In Karnataka, Congress-JD(S) Coalition on Brink as 13 MLAs Resign', *The Indian Express*, 7 July 2019, https://indianexpress.com/article/india/in-karnataka-congress-jds-coalition-on-brink-as-14-mlas-resign-5818975/, accessed 13 December 2021.

[4] 'Kamal Nath Resigns Ahead of Floor Test', *The Wire*, 20 March 2020, https://thewire.in/politics/floor-test-mp-resignation-16-rebel-congress-mla, accessed 13 December 2021.

[5] (1992) Supp (2) SCC 651. In this case, custodial validity of the Tenth Schedule was assailed. A constitution bench delivered its verdict on 18 February 1992.

for it said that the courts cannot even examine the decisions of the Speaker. The Supreme Court said that though it is for the Speaker to decide on the question of disqualification based on the discretionary power vested with him, the scope of judicial review cannot be erased. It is Clause 6 of the Tenth Schedule that empowers the Chairman or the Speaker of the House to decide on the question of disqualification. Very often, the Speaker's action or inaction has invited judicial intervention. As men of political parties, they have often delayed decisions or refused to decide issues fairly.

Before the Supreme Court, on 6 April 2021, the Goa Assembly Speaker through his lawyer agreed to pass final orders in the matter of disqualification of legislators who left the Congress to join the BJP and thereafter rejected the petition seeking to disqualify twelve members of the Assembly.[6] The disqualification petition on the ground of alleged defection was filed in 2019, and it took about eighteen months to get a decision on it. In the judgment in *Keisham Meghachandra Singh v. The Hon'ble Speaker Manipur* (2020),[7] a Supreme Court bench led by R.F. Nariman brooded over the impartiality of the Speakers and even said that 'Parliament may seriously consider amending the Constitution to substitute the Speaker of the Lok Sabha and Legislative Assemblies as arbiter of disputes concerning disqualification . . . with a permanent Tribunal'.

There is a view that sometimes legislators may have to act in accordance with their conscience. But the top court did not accept this contention in the *Kihoto Hollohan* case. We are yet to have a new generation of our 'Republicans' voting against Donald Trump, in protest against the Capitol riot.[8] In the US, UK, Germany and several other European countries, legislators are given the freedom of conscience. Even in India, prior to the incorporation of the Tenth Schedule, many lawmakers of the Congress who disagreed with Mrs Gandhi on her stand on the Emergency (1975–77) could express their dissent without fear of disqualification. This 'free speech' argument also has some relevance.

Defection in India, by and large, is synonymous with corruption. The

---

[6] 'Goa Speaker rejects plea to disqualify 12 MLAs', *The Indian Express*, 21 April 2021, https://indianexpress.com/article/india/goa-speaker-rejects-plea-to-disqualify-12-mlas-7282239/, accessed on 13 December 2021.

[7] 2020 SCC OnLine SC 55.

[8] In the US House of Representatives, thirty-five Republicans voted alongside the Democrats in support of the demand for enquiry into the riots of 6 January 2021, allegedly designed and executed by Trump supporters. See 'Trump Slams "Wayward" Republicans for Capitol Riot Vote', *BBC News*, 20 May 2021, https://www.bbc.com/news/world-us-canada-57180679, accessed 13 December 2021.

anti-defection laws by themselves cannot prevent defection when done by resignation, or sometimes by mere absence at the time of a confidence motion. With this understanding, the law on defection needs to be rewritten and an independent mechanism should be designed. In the process, free flow of ideas of the legislators also can be ensured in such a way that it does not amount to unfair political practice.

The New Indian Express, 12 April 2021, https://www.newindianexpress.com/opinions/ 2021/apr/12/defection-corruption-and-the-law-2288865.html.

34. Poll Panel Needs Radical Reforms

Electoral reforms should start with reforming the Election Commission (EC). The question is whether a regime that uses the EC for its immediate electoral gains will ever try to improve it, in the larger interest of democracy. Perhaps an activist judiciary will be able to revamp the EC.

O N 6 MAY 2021 a Supreme Court bench consisting of Justices D.Y. Chandrachud and M.R. Shah delivered a significant judgment. The court considered the plea by the Election Commission (EC) that sought to expunge certain oral observations of the Madras High Court against it. The Madras High Court, while considering a Covid-19-related case, said that the EC was singularly liable for the second wave of the pandemic by failing to regulate crowds during the election and should probably face murder charges.

The media reported these observations. The EC was aggrieved by these oral strictures and the media reports about them. The Supreme Court rightly rejected the plea by holding that institutions such as the EC are not immune from criticism. 'Our public constitutional institutions must find better responses than to complain', the court said. It also said that freedom of speech extends to reporting of judicial proceedings. Further: 'It would be retrograde for this court to promote the rule of law and access to justice on the one hand and shield the daily operations of the High Courts and this court from the media in all its forms by gagging the reporting of proceedings, on the other.'

In addition to seeking expunging of remarks, the Election Commission asked for some form of media censorship as well, as far as court reporting is concerned. Although the court rejected this demand, this conduct of the commission is an extension of its recent backsliding as a constitutional body. The EC has been accused of subserving those holding power at the centre. The institution is criticized for alleged political bias and partisanship. It faces a serious trust deficit.

We have two basic enactments dealing with elections – The Representation of the People Acts of 1950 and 1951. The EC has a pivotal role under both legislations. The Act of 1950 deals with delimitation of constituencies, preparation of electoral roll, etc. The latter enactment deals with the conduct of elections. Section 125 of this statute contains a significant warning. It penalizes persons promoting enmity between classes, in connection with election, on grounds of religion, community, etc. It is a statutory deterrent against using hate to solicit votes. The law encompasses many such activities and labels them as punishable offences. Preventing the offence is a sound forensic principle. Viewed as such, the EC must act as a constant guard for maintaining a healthy democracy.

One can see that coalition politics in India gave better functional autonomy to the EC. The period between 1989 and 2014 illustrates this point. This was a period of least governmental interference in the affairs of the EC, which in turn helped it to act as a free and fair umpire during elections. The Centre for the Study of Developing Societies (CSDS), Delhi, in a 1996 survey, found that the EC had captured the people's trust and even the judiciary in India came only next to it, in terms of public's faith.[1] The nation witnessed the proactive impartiality of T.N. Seshan, for whom the implementation of the Model Code of Conduct was an integral part of any election. His tenure (1990–96) conveyed the message of free and fair elections to the public at large. The point, however, is that systemic deficits cannot be rectified by the emergence of individuals.

After the resurrection of the majoritarianism, political parties used religious feelings as an easy and effective tool to canvass votes. The Commission failed to check hate speech in (and since) 2014 when the BJP got a majority in the Lok Sabha. The Congress, too, had played foul many a time when it enjoyed an absolute majority. But due to an active judiciary and better ethics in politics during the period following Independence, the institutional damage to the EC was minimal. It has no police force of its own. It has no 'purse or sword'. For the conduct of elections, the Commission must depend upon central forces and the state police.

The 2021 Bengal election was marred by hate as a political device, for which the innocent public had to pay a heavy cost even in terms of their lives. Formed in 1950, the EC has travelled a long and difficult path since then. The body is chosen by the executive. The irony is direct and embarrassing – an appointee by a majoritarian executive is expected to act judiciously and independently when confronted with political parties. This is a fundamental flaw in the design of the EC.

A free and fair process to select the EC is therefore an imperative for the

---

[1] Manjari Katju, 'Election Commission and Functioning of Democracy', *Economic and Political Weekly*, vol. 41, no. 17, 29 April 2006, https://www.epw.in/journal/2006/17/perspectives/election-commission-and-functioning-democracy.html, accessed 13 December 2021.

fulfilment of its role as a neutral arbiter. An assertive EC should be politically non-affiliative. It is also essential to minimize the EC's dependence on the executive for doing its constitutional duty. An independent law-enforcing agency as visualized by the Supreme Court in the *Prakash Singh* case (2006), indicated in chapter 30, can go a long way to ensure functional autonomy for the EC. In the *Vineet Narain* case (1997), also noted in chapter 30, the Supreme Court evolved a select panel consisting of the Prime Minister, the Home Minister and the leader of the opposition for choosing the Central Vigilance Commissioner 'from a panel of outstanding civil servants and others with impeccable integrity, to be furnished by the Cabinet Secretary'.

Likewise, a better select body was suggested to choose the CBI Director as well. The selection of the EC needs to have a representative, divergent and participative character. In his classic work, journalist Philip Coggan explained the crisis faced by democracies in the west. His book had a cautioning title: 'The Last Vote'.[2] Electoral reforms in India need to begin with reimagining the EC. It should be revamped both structurally and functionally to preserve our electoral democracy.

The New Indian Express, 9 May 2021, https://www.newindianexpress.com/opinions/2021/may/09/poll-panel-needs-radical-reforms-2300107.html

---

[2] Philip Coggan, *The Last Vote*, London: Allen Lane, 2013.

35. Manifestos and Judicial Reforms

This article was published on the eve of the 2019 general elections to the Indian Parliament. Concerns of judicial reforms seldom find a place in the manifestos of political parties or among the voters. This reflects poorly on our priorities. The institutional deficit of the judicial system is perpetuated by this apathy as well.

'JUDGES DO NOT HAVE an easy job. They repeatedly do what the rest of us seek to avoid; make decisions', said the famous British lawyer David Pannick in his celebrated work, *Judges*.[1] The point, however, is not somehow to make decisions. A society needs fair, just and timely decisions, for which an impartial and independent judiciary is a democratic imperative. A 'committed' judiciary is a threat to the constitutional ethos, and in the Indian context, it demonstrated the darkest era after Independence.

All is not well with the Indian courts. We have a faulty and opaque system for the selection and appointment of judges to the higher judiciary. Lack of judicial accountability has often led to patent arbitrariness in adjudication. Instances of judicial misbehaviour and corruption are not uncommon. The law's delays are notorious. Litigation becomes the privilege of the rich, especially in societies where socio-economic inequality is the rule. Lawyers are sometimes assessed by the money that they earn, rather than the quality of their work. A new legal plutocracy has emerged in the country. As former SC judge J. Chelameswar once put it, mediocrity remains a great threat to India's legal system, when the choice for the bench and selection of the leaders of the bar are done based on 'impressions rather than evaluation'.

The question during the 2019 Lok Sabha elections is how far our political parties are able to address the issues of judicial independence and standard of justice. An examination of the poll manifestos reveals interesting contradictions and disturbing deficits. The National Democratic Alliance (NDA) government, by its historic move to introduce the National Judicial Appointments Commission (NJAC), had at least attempted to put an end to the collegium system in the country whereby judges are essentially appointed by judges, by not following a fair procedure. The proposed NJAC, though not adequately representative or participative as it should have been, was a

---

[1] David Pannick, *Judges*, Oxford: Oxford University Press, 1988.

radical step to put an end to the vices of collegium. But the 99th Constitutional Amendment that aimed at a relatively independent commission was stalled by the top court by its judgment of 16 October 2015. The legislation was struck down. The verdict does not, however, mean that the Parliament or the political executive at the centre needs to abandon the reformative agenda forever. There is a need to reconceptualize the Commission, by erasing the possibility for political domination that was perceived as a threat to judicial independence.

Strangely, the BJP's manifesto makes only a casual reference to judicial reforms. Ironically, it is silent about the present method of appointment of judges by way of the collegium system. Chapter 9 clause 7 of the manifesto says: 'We will work towards simplifying procedure laws, encouraging mediation and strengthening judicial and court management system in order to increase accessibility.' The manifesto of the Congress is richer in details but poorer in terms of credibility. Chapter 29 of its poll manifesto promises a National Judicial Commission (NJC). It says: 'The NJC will be comprised of judges, jurists and parliamentarians and will be serviced by a Secretariat. Names of suitable candidates will be placed in the public domain.' Also, it offers to constitute a Judicial Complaints Commission 'to investigate complaints of misconduct against judges and recommend suitable action to Parliament'.

The fact of the matter is that the Congress, while in power, could not make any successful legislation to bring in any significant change. It did not strive for an independent selection committee at all, while its effort by way of the Judicial Standard and Accountability Bill passed in Lok Sabha in March 2012 lapsed with the dissolution of the 15th Lok Sabha in 2014.

In Canada, a new system was designed by Prime Minister Justin Trudeau that enabled all qualified persons to apply for judicial posts in the top courts. That ensured equality of opportunity in judicial appointments by way of a fair and transparent process. Equality leads to quality.

At present, the judges of the constitutional courts are predominantly selected from among the advocates. A lawyer's job is fundamentally different from that of a judge. A change could be worth considering. Article 124(3)(c) of the Constitution contemplates selection of a Supreme Court judge from among 'distinguished jurists' as well. This provision is yet to find its proper implementation. At the least, instead of selecting lawyers from the same state as judges of the High Court, those from other states could be a better option. But the method of selection needs to be democratized by ensuring equality of opportunity.

Juridical reform is no longer a legal issue pertaining to a few lawyers or judges. It is a political issue that concerns the public in the republic, and therefore should find a place in the electoral discourse. The political parties in India need to address the deficits in the legal system more comprehensively with a sense of statesmanship. As stated by Justice Warren Burger, 'the notion that ordinary people want black-robed judges, well-dressed lawyers and fine-panelled court rooms as the setting to resolve their disputes is not correct. People with problems, like people with pain, want relief, and they want it as quickly and inexpensively as possible.'[2]

The New Indian Express, 17 April 2019, https://www.newindianexpress.com/opinions/2019/apr/17/manifestos-and-judicial-reforms-1965363.html.

---

[2] As cited in Oscar G. Chase and Jonathan Thong, 'Judging Judges: The Effect of Courtroom Ceremony on Participant Evaluation of Process Fairness-Related Factors', *Yale Journal of Law and the Humanities*, vol. 24, no. 1, 2013, p. 222.

36. Governance During the Pandemic

The Covid-19 pandemic in India provided economic, political and legal lessons. The nation's experience during the tough times should act as a reminder for the future. History does its course correction by recapitulating tragedies.

CRISES REVEAL THE capacity of the state and the quality of governance. The Covid-19 pandemic in India has killed lakhs of people across the country. The corpses found floating in the Ganges in the months of May and June 2021[1] exposed the emptiness of our rhetoric on development and underlined the harsh Indian reality. Human dignity suffered in life as well as in death. Article 21 of the Constitution, talking about the right to life, appeared a dead letter. More than a health crisis, we are in a political crisis, a civilizational crisis. Belatedly, the centre has come out with a new vaccination policy. It decided to procure 75 per cent of the vaccine doses and to allot the same to the states so as to enable the states to carry out free vaccination. According to the initial policy, the burden to purchase vaccine from the manufacturers was on the state governments. The direction of the top court and criticism from the public had some impact.

Laws are devices to be used appropriately in critical situations as a means of social engineering. The state can use its laws for the betterment of the people or to their detriment. It can use or misuse its offices, and choose to help or punish its citizens. Two aspects were notable in the conduct of the executive: a lack of accountability and a convenient misuse of the pandemic period.

Certain restrictions like enforced physical distancing might be valid and necessary in view of the health crisis. But the pandemic cannot give *carte blanche* to the government to do as it pleases without accountability or legitimacy. Literature on freedom during the time of Covid-19 makes for a wonderful read. Some references in this regard are made in chapter 22. In a

---

[1] The international media widely reported this shocking chain of events. See Geeta Pandey, 'Covid-19: India's Holiest River is Swollen with Bodies', *BBC News*, 19 May 2021, available at https://www.bbc.com/news/world-asia-india-57154564, accessed 23 December 2021. Also see Saurabh Sharma, 'Poverty, Stigma Behind Bodies Floating in India's Ganges River', *Al Jazeera*, 2 June 2021, available at https://www.aljazeera.com/news/2021/6/2/poverty-stigma-behind-bodies-floating-in-indias-ganges-river, accessed 23 December 2021.

recent essay, Leslie Francis rightly points out that the court is concerned with
the question of whether 'the public health interest is sufficiently strong to
override presumed individual liberties'.[2] During an epidemic, the state can
take away one's freedom to form a crowd. But it cannot book somebody for
being a whistle-blower. It cannot shoot the messenger because the message is
unpleasant to the government.

Throughout the pandemic, till the court actively intervened, the centre
showed little or no seriousness in the matter. A bench headed by Justice
D.Y. Chandrachud on 30 April 2021 asked if the centre had ever considered
invoking Sections 92 and 100 of the Patents Act, and issuing compulsory
licenses to the firms to ensure adequate production and supply of vaccines.
These provisions are meant to be used during a health emergency. Also, these
are provisions that work against monopolization of production, which the
country cannot afford right now. On 31 May, the same bench asked the
centre to place its vaccine policy before the court. The court also asked how
the budget allocation of Rs 35,000 crore has been spent so far and why it
cannot be used for the vaccination programme. A division bench of the
Kerala High Court asked why a part of the enormous surplus money that
the Reserve Bank granted to the centre cannot be utilized for vaccination.
It required the court to tell the executive and the legislature as to how they
should act and correct themselves. Democracy always needs judicial vigilance
and executive sensitivity.

The international media also questioned the nation's policies relating
to the pandemic. Economists, academics and writers have widely written
about what could be done differently to improve lives in a health crisis. In
a democracy, criticisms are measures to keep the executive under check. The
announcement of the new vaccine policy demonstrates this principle.

One would expect the executive to be prepared with responses and
expertise since they fall within the exclusive domain of its policy. The centre's
reaction initially was characterized by ill-equipped approaches and failure of
governance. It was also intolerant towards any dissent and was more interested
in suppressing criticism than assessing its merit.

The government also made use of the pandemic period to evade the
consultative process and clamp down on civil liberties. The centre's hurry
to implement the Citizenship (Amendment) Act in an indirect way is an
example. It issued a notification on 28 May 2021 inviting the minorities

[2] Leslie Francis, 'Negative Freedom in Crisis Times', *Utah Law Digital Commons*, SJ
Quinney College of Law, University of Utah, 2021.

in Afghanistan, Bangladesh and Pakistan to seek Indian citizenship. This happened while the matter is pending before the Supreme Court and when the rules under the Act are yet to be framed. This also shows the priority of the executive at a time when there is enormous suffering in a health emergency.

The administrator's action in Lakshadweep curtailing the freedom of the islanders is yet another instance (see the next chapter for details). Even before the enactment of draft regulations and laws, protesters in the island were arrested and detained, though for a short while. The islanders say that they have not been consulted prior to the drastic changes about to be implemented, altering the future of the island.

All these and many other episodes displayed a spiteful state. A responsible government ought to have concentrated on the war against the virus rather than against the people. The Constitution, by way of the Directive Principles, which are frequently referred to in this book, provides for a blueprint for governance with a sense of compassion and fraternity. Article 38 persuades the state to 'eliminate inequalities in status, facilities, and opportunities'. Article 39 dreams about equitable distribution of resources. It dislikes 'concentration of wealth and means of production to the common detriment'. This could presently mean encouraging a large number of firms to produce vaccines for a cheaper price and ensuring free access to it. Even Article 51A(h) incorporated during the Emergency has a contextual relevance. It appeals 'to develop the scientific temper, humanism and spirit of inquiry'. The Prime Minister of the country cannot therefore ask the people to beat plates as a means to eradicate the virus.

To overcome the pandemic, the government needs to better prepare with adequate health expenditure and a well-defined policy. It should also ensure just and equitable implementation of the revised vaccine policy.

The New Indian Express, 9 June 2021, https://www.newindianexpress.com/opinions/2021/jun/09/governance-during-the-pandemic-2313489.html.

37. Lakshadweep: When the Law Unsettles Everything

The actions of the administrator of the Union Territory of Lakshadweep in 2021 are an alarm call for the whole nation. The centre should be just and fair in governing its territories.

'SMALL IS BEAUTIFUL' is the title of E.F. Schumacher's famous book published in 1973. He was an economist and in his seminal work, he talked about fairer economic policies with smaller and appropriate technology. Lakshadweep, to a good extent, embodied his philosophy. The island is unique and wonderful – ecologically, culturally, geographically and economically. As an archipelago of thirty-six islands with a total extent of only 32 sq km, this terrain is India's smallest Union Territory.[1] Its literacy rate is 91.85 per cent,[2] very close to that of Kerala where it is 96.2 per cent.[3] It has ten village panchayats.[4] Only ten of the islands are inhabited, and the total population is only around 64,473.[5] The crime rate is very low according to the 2019 report of the National Crime Records Bureau. There was not even a single Covid-19 case reported in 2020. The health index is generally good.

In 2021, the island was in the news. Nefarious schemes formulated by the Lakshadweep administration have turned the sense of comfort upside down. As history shows, bad politics often manifests through bad laws, and the island is no exception. Lakshadweep has no legislative assembly. Article 239 of the Constitution says that Union Territories are to be administered by the President through an administrator appointed by him, if there is no law to the contrary. Laws are proposed and promulgated by the administration.

The centre, through the administration, has come up with four draft regulations in 2021: The Lakshadweep Development Authority Regulation, The Prevention of Anti-Social Activities (PASA) Regulation, The Lakshadweep Animal Preservation Regulation and The Lakshadweep Panchayat Regulation.

---

[1] Official website of the U.T. Administration of Lakshadweep, https://lakshadweep.gov.in/, accessed 23 December 2021.

[2] Ibid.

[3] Official website of Kerala State Literacy Mission Authority, https://literacy missionkerala.org/en/at-96-2-kerala-tops-literacy-rate-chart-andhra-pradesh-worst-performer/, accessed 23 December 2021.

[4] https://lakshadweep.gov.in/, accessed 23 December 2021.

[5] Ibid.

The so-called 'development' regulation fails to honour the people's basic rights over land. The draft law proposes 'town planning' for which a Planning and Development Authority (PDA) will be constituted, as per Section 7. The development plan will be imposed upon the people from the top. This is dramatically opposite to the system of the village panchayat having a pivotal role in designing the future of the island. Wajahat Habibullah, a retired bureaucrat who was the administrator of the island during 1987–90, said in a recent article that the Union Territory had a decentralized system by which 'the Island Development Council, at the apex of the local government, was mandated to advise the administrator on development'.[6] As part of the development plan, the whole terrain comes under the control of the authority as per Section 18. The land allocation, its use, demarcation of zones, construction, reallocation of people, control of almost everything from architectural features to agricultural land, all become the prerogative of the government or the authority. Section 71 gives power to the PDA for removal or demolition of buildings in the areas covered under the scheme. Section 72 empowers the district magistrate to summarily evict the occupants in the scheme-covered areas. Section 119 is drastic as it contemplates imprisonment of the 'obstructers' of the scheme for a period up to two months, apart from imposition of a fine.

The right to property is no longer a fundamental right in India. Article 19(1)(f), which promised this right, was deleted with effect from 20 June 1979. However, for the indigenous tribes in a natural habitat, the right to land is a fundamental right. This proposition was laid down by the Supreme Court in *Samatha v. State of Andhra Pradesh* (1997).[7] About 94.8 per cent of the island's population are Scheduled Tribes.[8] More than 94 per cent of the persons who hold land in the islands are members of Scheduled Tribes.[9] Therefore, going by the geographic, ethnic and environmental features, the draconian regulation, despite its legal rhetoric on development, cannot pass constitutional muster.

The penal provisions in the PASA draft regulation are also worth

---

[6] Wajahat Habibullah, 'A "Reform Wave" Lakshadweep Could Do Without', *The Hindu*, 31 May 2021, https://www.thehindu.com/opinion/lead/a-reform-wave-lakshadweep-could-do-without/article34684315.ece, accessed 23 December 2021.

[7] (1997) 8 SCC 191.

[8] Census of India, *Lakshadweep Series-32 Part XII-B District Census Handbook Lakshadweep*, 2011, https://censusindia.gov.in/2011census/dchb/3101_PART_B_DCHB_LAKSHADWEEP.pdf, accessed 23 December 2021.

[9] Aditi Murti, 'Lakshadweep's New Land Reforms Threaten Its Fragile Ecosystems, Citizen Rights', *The Swaddle*, 25 May 2021, https://theswaddle.com/lakshadweeps-new-land-reforms-threaten-its-fragile-ecosystems-citizen-rights/, accessed 23 December 2021.

examining. Perhaps their very purpose is to suppress the protest that the administration anticipates while proposing the anti-democratic laws. The draft contemplates preventive detention, by way of Section 3. Detention based on a vague, non-existent or irrelevant charge is sought to be validated by Section 6. When the fertility rate in the island is much less than the country's average, the disqualification of those with more than two children to get elected to the panchayat does not make sense, though it would serve a communal agenda. More importantly, such a provision is *per se* undemocratic and inhuman. So is the case with the anti-cow slaughter proposal. The anti-minority hate campaign in the mainland by Hindutva outfits was sought to be intensified with such designs in the Muslim-dominated island.

The island is ecologically fragile. A recent study by scientists at IIT Kharagpur says that the rise in sea levels between 0.4 mm and 0.9 mm annually might lead to coastal erosion and even submergence of some of the islets.[10] Climate change impacts the island ecology more quickly and manifestly. Coral reefs are already destroyed immensely due to mindless 'developmental' activities. An appeal by a group of scientists said that the development plan in the island ignores India's basic environmental legislations, like the Environment Protection Act (1986) and the Biodiversity Act (2002). The idea of an Environment Impact Assessment for major projects has its genesis in the 1986 enactment. The Justice Raveendran Committee Report 2014, prepared at the behest of the Supreme Court, is also crucial for the island. It contains a plea for the conservation of corals, lagoons and other habitats. The report puts forward a comprehensive plan dealing with topics like coconut plantation and deep-sea fishing. The change of land use and provision for a new pattern of development now proposed go against ecological sanity.

Legislation is too serious a matter to be left to the legislators alone and much less to the administrators. Consultation with the local people only improves the law's democratic legitimacy. For that, we need statesmen rather than politicians. The pity, however, is that sometimes we don't have politicians, but only traders at the helm of affairs.

The New Indian Express, 2 August 2021, https://www.newindianexpress.com/opinions/2021/aug/02/legislative-immunity-is-not-absolute-2338753.html.

---

[10] Esha Roy, 'Lakshadweep Could Face Major Coastal Erosion Due to Rising Sea Levels: Study', *The Indian Express*, 22 June 2021, https://indianexpress.com/article/india/lakshadweep-could-face-major-coastal-erosion-due-to-rising-sea-levels-study-7369707/, accessed 23 December 2021.

38. Targeted Surveillance: A Threat to Democracy

It was after the publication of this article that the Supreme Court issued an interim order on 27 October 2021 in Manohar Lal Sharma v. Union of India and Ors. (2021) *on the Pegasus issue.[1] The court formed a technical committee to be overseen by Justice R. V. Raveendran, former judge of the Supreme Court of India. The terms of reference of the committee include enquiry into the alleged use of Pegasus spyware on Indian citizens, details of the victims of the spyware and the steps taken by the government after the reports about hacking in 2019.[2] The committee's interim report is now before the court.*

THE PEGASUS CASE poses an unprecedented challenge to India, hinting at the emergence of surveillance across countries in furtherance to a global conspiracy that has scant regard for democracies or institutions elsewhere. The future will depend upon how the nation and its institutions respond to it.

The appointment of the Justice Lokur Commission by the West Bengal government was a sensible and pragmatic move. However, the activities of the Commission have been stayed by the Supreme Court in view of its decision to form a technical committee.[3] As of 5 August 2021, the Supreme Court of India had heard the initial submissions on behalf of the petitioners in the slew of litigations seeking a probe into the shocking surveillance. The Chief Justice said that the allegations were serious. The court asked why the registration of first information reports (FIRs) had not been sought for at the individual level, that is, at the instance of the complainants. In a case of targeted surveillance where revelations from credible sources have come out only recently, the request to the apex court for taking judicial cognizance of the issue is sensible.

It is significant to note that the technical committee formed by the Supreme Court has only started to function. Even as it works and even as it submits its report, the country needs to vigilantly follow up the issue. The court also will have to oversee the matter throughout so as to carry forward the tough task that it has undertaken. This article tries to lay down a thematic premise for our concerns regarding surveillance.

---

[1] *Manohar Lal Sharma v. Union of India and Ors.* (2021), SCC OnLine SC 985.
[2] Ibid.
[3] Ibid.

Given the fact that the political executive has been adopting a posture of egregious silence and that no debate on the issue has been permitted on the floors of both Houses of Parliament, the court may have to carry out its function of scanning the issue judicially with reference to the various legal, constitutional and political issues highlighted in the petitions.

Threat to Democracy

According to reports, the spyware has targeted not merely the leaders of the formal opposition or those who are part of government institutions in India. Several public intellectuals and activists, too, are in the list. This has happened at a time when many dissidents of the regime have been labelled as 'anti-nationals' and put in prison for indefinite periods. They have been denied bail principally on account of the terrorist/anti-national tag which the government foisted on them.

The irony is that the Pegasus allegations essentially point to the anti-national posture taken by the government and those who run it. The attempts made by them to hush up the episode has only aggravated concerns. As Arundhati Roy put it, 'there has to be something treasonous about a foreign corporation servicing and maintaining a spy network that is monitoring a country's private citizens on behalf of that country's government'.[4] The total lack of moral authority of a regime that invoked draconian legal provisions in order to witch-hunt its citizens by questioning their patriotism is now clearly under the scanner at a very foundational level.

It is on record that the NSO group of Israel said that it sells the software technology 'solely to law enforcement and intelligence agencies of vetted governments'.[5] Therefore, there is a formal and institutional character to the deal. The role of private players will also be serious, though it might be under the garb of the instrumentalities of the state. Given the very nature of the alleged hacking, the individuals involved can only be those at the helm of affairs in one capacity or the other. Therefore, the issue is no longer at the level of individual crime.

No doubt, at a narrow and personal level, the allegation will point to the infiltration of telephonic devices and unauthorized surveillance. This would

[4] Arundhati Roy, 'Only Political Action can Mitigate the Disastrous Effects of Pegasus Spyware', *The Wire*, 27 July 2021, accessed 24 December 2021.
[5] 'Pegasus Issue: Governments Need to Hold NSO Accountable: WhatsApp CEO', *The Hindu*, 20 July 2021, accessed 24 December 2021.

fall within the ambit of the Indian Telegraph Act, 1885 and the Information Technology Act, 2000, and certain provisions in the Indian Penal Code (IPC). But any serious concern over the issue will necessarily take this as an attack on the nation, its institutions, citizens and democracy in multiple ways. The culpable silence of the regime that allegedly tried to betray its people is inexcusable and least convincing.

The fact that as many as 174 persons were allegedly potential targets in India[6] indicates the political and institutional nature of the conspiracy. Did the government or its agencies seek the spyware service? This is essentially the question that every enlightened citizen is bound to ask. It does not arise out of speculation based on hearsay. A consortium of seventeen media houses across the world, in collaboration with the French news organization Forbidden Stories, with technical assistance from Amnesty International, came out with credible and legitimate reports.[7] Many have also pointed to the political bond between Prime Minister Narendra Modi and the erstwhile President of Israel, Benjamin Netanyahu, by focusing on the proximity between Modi's visit to Israel and the period of the alleged snooping. The widespread and multifaceted nature of the issue with international ramifications calls for an independent and effective investigation into this global digital crime. As the journalist M.K. Venu wrote: 'Only a genuine probe, both at the national and global level, would reveal the true extent of use of Pegasus. Any journalistic venture is limited by resources and its investigations can only give strong evidentiary pointers to a bigger transgression.'[8] The petitions before the Supreme Court seek such a probe. The opposition in both Houses of Parliament also demands the same. The court's intervention has facilitated it.

THE LEGAL LANDSCAPE

In *People's Union for Civil Liberties (PUCL) v. Union of India* (1996),[9] the apex court analysed the scope as well as the limitations of Section 5(2) of the

---

[6] 'Pegasus Project: 174 Individuals Revealed by The Wire On Snoop List So Far', *The Wire*, 4 August 2021, https://thewire.in/rights/project-pegasus-list-of-names-uncovered-spyware-surveillance, accessed 24 December 2021.

[7] Phineas Rueckert, 'Pegasus: The New Global Weapon for Silencing Journalists', *Forbidden Stories*, 18 July 2021, https://forbiddenstories.org/pegasus-the-new-global-weapon-for-silencing-journalists/, accessed 24 December 2021.

[8] M.K. Venu, 'How Long Can India Ignore the Ramifications of the Pegasus Scandal?', *The Wire*, 29 July 2021, accessed 24 December 2021.

[9] (1997) 1 SCC 301.

Indian Telegraph Act, 1885. This is a pre-constitutional enactment that does not jurisprudentially enjoy the moral legitimacy of a post-constitutional law, for it was enacted by the colonial regime without parliamentary debate.

But the striking feature of the law is that despite its colonial vintage, it imposes heavy restrictions on the state's power to interrupt or detain or prohibit telegraphic (electronic) communication. It is permissible only 'on the occurrence of any public emergency or in the interest of the public safety'. The government should satisfy the requirement to do so for reasons related to national security, public order, prevention of crimes and so on. Any interception, or actions akin to that, can happen only by an order where the reasons are to be recorded. Even according to the colonial law, an act of interception must be preceded by a due process with a great sense of accountability. The provision clarifies that for press messages, transmission is the rule, and interception or detention can occur only when there is an express prohibition under Section 5(2) of the Act.

Understanding these safeguards in the context of the snooping that has allegedly taken place now would be highly instructive. In the PUCL case, the Supreme Court said that the right to privacy, though 'by itself has not been identified' under the Constitution, is part of the right to life and personal liberty enshrined under Article 21 of the Constitution. A striking feature of the judgment is that it read the pre-constitutional statute constitutionally. The statute, too, facilitated such a reading by its own content. The court, while analysing the terms of Section 5(2) of the Indian Telegraph Act, gave it a more restrictive meaning and thereby indicated that a public emergency cannot be conceived merely on the basis of a unilateral assertion by the government that does not stand to reason.

When the PUCL case was decided, India was yet to have a comprehensive law on data protection. The Information Technology Act (IT Act) came into effect from 17 October 2000, and was substantially amended many times. This special enactment makes hacking an offence. Chapter XI of the Act talks about different offences under the Act. It includes tampering (Section 65), identity theft (Section 66-C), violation of privacy (Section 66-E) and so on. Section 66-E gives an extremely narrow definition of privacy by limiting it to the private parts of a person's body. These provisions on their own are insufficient to deal with the issues involved in the Pegasus case.

Yet, significantly, Section 66-F of the IT Act talks about 'cyberterrorism', for which punishment up to imprisonment for life is prescribed. Going by the language of Section 66-F, even an attempt at an unauthorized penetration or access to computer resource that goes against the sovereignty and integrity of

India or the security of the state is a serious offence. Such cybercrimes against the national interest could be committed by those running the state as well, both definitionally and practically. The allegations related to Pegasus *prima facie* indicate such activities were allegedly carried out by using the state machinery, taking advantage of the apparatus that India's own democracy provided to such persons responsible.

TESTING MOMENT FOR *PUTTASWAMY* CASE

It is essential to notice the famous rewriting of the law that happened in *Justice K.S. Puttaswamy (Retd) v. Union of India* in 2017,[10] which is bound to have a precedential value that the apex court cannot ignore while deciding the Pegasus list. Justice Y.V. Chandrachud, as part of the majority in the infamous *ADM Jabalpur v. Shivkant Shukla* case in 1976,[11] endorsed the suspension of fundamental rights during the Emergency (1975–77). He said in the judgment that 'the right to personal liberty has no hallmark'. According to him, the express provisions on fundamental rights in the Constitution do not make them absolute and unalterable because what is provided by the Constitution can also be annulled by it. He said: 'It is impossible to identify whether the right is one given by the Constitution or is one which existed in the pre-Constitution era.' Without any such dilemma, Justice H.R. Khanna, in his seminal dissent, said: 'Even in the absence of Article 21 in the Constitution, the state has got no power to deprive a person of his life or liberty without the authority of law.' In the *Puttaswamy* case, D.Y. Chandrachud, as part of a nine-judge bench, categorically said that 'the judgments rendered by all the four judges constituting the majority in *ADM Jabalpur* are seriously flawed'. Thus, the *Puttaswamy* case has overruled the highly disillusioning and dreadful proposition in the *ADM Jabalpur* case that blatantly supported executive high-handedness.

The impact of the *Puttaswamy* case in the Pegasus case must be in this more fundamental fashion. The question of targeted surveillance needs to be constitutionally addressed on the basis of the liberal platform laid down in the *Puttaswamy* case, in contradistinction with the 'seriously flawed' proposition in *ADM Jabalpur*. This writer has indicated that the pragmatic value of the verdict in the *Puttaswamy* case will have to be tested in concrete political

---

[10] (2017) 10 SCC 1.
[11] (1976) 2 SCC 521.

situations and not merely at the doctrinal level.[12] Though the *Puttaswamy* case has repeatedly been relied upon in many litigations across the country in the context of various dimensions of the right to privacy, the Pegasus case could prove to be a clear testing moment for the judgment.

Privacy becomes a fundamental value since it pertains to the liberty, dignity and autonomy of an individual, as recognized in the *Puttaswamy* case. More importantly, the reliance on privacy is also an assertion against an aggrandizing and intruding state. Privacy is a communitarian and political idea, which too was recognized in clear terms in the *Puttaswamy* case. In the words of Justice D.Y. Chandrachud, 'privacy is the constitutional core of human dignity'. The United States Supreme Court in *Katz v. United States* (1967)[13] explained that the Fourth Amendment to the US Constitution ensures a 'reasonable expectation of privacy'. Unlike the US, the Indian Constitution does not specifically talk about privacy as a fundamental right. Therefore, in the *Puttaswamy* case, it is by way of a judicial synthesis and adopting an organic approach to the Constitution, instead of textually reading it, that the Supreme Court explained privacy. It implied in so many words that in India, privacy is also a political right.

The legal challenges that Pegasus poses to India and inside India are unique and, to a good extent, unprecedented. They are not related to mere crimes at the individual or international level. The issue hints at the emergence of targeted surveillance in furtherance to a global conspiracy that has scant regard for democracies or institutions elsewhere. It can pose a threat to the media, civil society movements, political protests, and the functioning of institutions including the Cabinet, the judiciary, the bureaucracy and the legislature. There are reasons to believe that the intrusion has something to do with certain cardinal decisions that impacted the nation. Many included in the list of targeted persons are connected or concerned with several major developments in the country, in the recent past.

When the PUCL case was decided, the court was dealing with a narrow compass of state-induced surveillance on the citizens. But the *Puttaswamy* case is drawn on a larger canvas which has the potential to address various facets of the Pegasus row. The neuroscientist-filmmaker Mauktik Kulkarni wrote: 'If true, the implications of such surveillance are not limited to political, bureaucratic, journalistic, or judicial opponents of the current government.

[12] Kaleeswaram Raj, 'Not an Honourable Track Record', *Frontline*, 24 November 2017.
[13] 389 US 347.

They will affect the economic climate, open-minded academic inquiry, and spirited debates among students and civil society, which are all essential for a thriving democracy.'[14]

The Pegasus issue poses an unprecedented challenge to India. The future will depend upon how the nation and its institutions respond to it. It is to be seen whether we will have yet another 'tryst with destiny', as Jawaharlal Nehru had famously put it.

Frontline, 27 August 2021, https://frontline.thehindu.com/cover-story/will-the-pegasus-case-be-another-tryst-with-destiny-for-india/article35809971.ece.

---

[14] Mauktik Kulkarni, 'Why Americans Should be Alarmed by the Pegasus Spyware Controversy in India', *Scroll.in*, 2 August 2021, accessed 24 December 2021.

39. Pegasus Order Calls for Cautious Optimism

As indicated in the previous chapter, across the world, targeted surveillance with a political agenda to fulfil the interests of market forces, or of those who run electoral autocracies, poses a civilizational threat. It is all the more so in India where a government runs the show with scant regard for individual rights. Here is a further analysis.

THE SUPREME COURT'S order constituting an expert committee to probe into the allegations on the use of the spyware is captivating. The accusation that the government has, in collaboration with a foreign company, snooped on its own people and institutions is perturbing. As the court indicated in its order on 27 October 2021, the constitutional and democratic concerns involved in the issue cannot be lost in the political thicket. Allegedly, thousands of devices were snooped all over the world. Persons working across various fields were named as victims of the surveillance.

After the *Puttaswamy* verdict (2017),[1] privacy rights were asserted before the Supreme Court in many cases. But in the instant case of *Manohar Lal Sharma v. Union of India* (2021),[2] the right to privacy is manifested in multiple forms in the personal and public lives of the citizens. As explained already, the very legitimacy of a regime that harshly used nationalism and patriotism to incarcerate the citizens is now clearly under a judicial scanner. At a time when the opposition in the country faces an existential dilemma, the court, with all its limits, asked certain inconvenient and tough questions.

The Orwellian concerns expressed in the court order go far beyond political parties and national boundaries. Illegal surveillance strikes at the root of the right to privacy. International targeted surveillance with a political agenda to fulfil the interests of the market forces, or of those who run the electoral autocracies, poses a civilizational threat to humankind. French philosopher Michel Foucault has explained the fundamental nexus between dictatorial power, surveillance and social control. In his memoir *Permanent Record* (2019), Edward Snowden[3] talks about 'surveillance capitalism' and the relevance of an 'international opposition movement'. He also indicates

---

[1] See chapter 28.
[2] (2021) SCC OnLine 985.
[3] Edward Snowden, *Permanent Record*, Macmillan, 2019.

the contradiction that the law is 'country-specific, whereas technology is not'. Therefore, it is essential to equip the laws to address the global and technical challenges involved in the Pegasus issue.

In the Supreme Court, the government did not specifically answer a short and straightforward question: whether or not it used Pegasus for surveillance. According to the provisions in the Civil Procedure Code, failure or refusal to clearly answer the 'point of substance' can invite adverse findings and consequences. In constitutional litigations, the government has a duty to reveal all the facts and information in its possession to the court, as stated in *Ram Jethmalani v. Union of India* (2011)[4] and reiterated in the present order of the court. More than a matter of law, this reflects an approach of prudence and common sense. The regime's silence on the point is noteworthy. It aggravated apprehensions about selective surveillance with a specific hidden agenda.

The public interest litigation (PIL) movement that gained momentum after the Emergency suffered a setback in recent times for multiple reasons. Lack of seriousness and procedural certainty, coupled with abuse of the jurisdiction, resulted in trivialization of the device. Anuj Bhuwania has elaborated on the problems and dangers that the institution of PIL posed in India in his seminal work, *Courting the People* (2017).[5] The order in the Pegasus case gives hope for the re-emergence of genuine and serious social action litigations.

The court order has an instructive and intrinsic value as well. Sometimes, constitutional courts can act as great public educators, though their primary function is different. The order says that in an ambience of surveillance, the press or the people cannot be free. The court traced the quintessential relation between freedom of expression and freedom from surveillance. In the words of the court, 'the knowledge that one is under the threat of being spied on can affect the way an individual decides to exercise his or her rights', and 'such a scenario might result in self-censorship'. Indisputably, surveillance is policing the thoughts, dreams and imagination of individuals and their collectives. It annihilates the freedom of the press in tremendous ways. It intimidates even the source of information, the foundation of the fourth estate. It is an egregious trespass into forbidden zones. The order is valuable for its authoritative emphasis on 'protection of journalistic sources'.

The challenges before the committee are enormous. If the government continues to adopt a stubborn attitude, as it did before the court, or does

[4] (2011) 8 SCC 1.
[5] Anuj Bhuwania, *Courting the People*, Cambridge University Press, 2017.

not cooperate in the steps ahead, timely and effective judicial interventions may be needed. The device called 'continuing mandamus', where the court constantly oversees the progress of the activities or lack of it, and issues directives from time to time, may turn out to be a processual imperative.

We need an effective mechanism to ensure cybersecurity for the nation. In the event of unauthorized intrusions, access to quick legal remedies should be guaranteed. Planting spyware in targeted devices and email accounts is an aggravated form of surveillance that warrants severe punishment.

But at the end of the day, the Pegasus litigation calls not only for judicial vigilance but alertness of the civil society at large. Digital surveillance has the potential to turn democracies upside down. As such, no one can live with a false notion of individual security. As writer Thor Benson reminds us: 'Don't oppose mass surveillance for your own sake. Oppose it for the activists, lawyers, journalists and all of the other people our liberty relies on.'

The New Indian Express, 15 Novemeber 2021, https://www.newindianexpress.com/opinions/columns/2021/nov/15/pegasus-order-calls-for-cautious-optimism-2383618.html

PART FIVE

ON LIFE

40. A Case Against the Death Penalty

The four accused in the Nirbhaya case – Pawan Gupta (25), Vinay Sharma (26), Akshay (31) and Mukesh (32) – were hanged to death on 20 March 2020. This article was written prior to their execution at Tihar Jail. It is essential to rethink how the Nirbhaya incident, where a 23-year-old girl was brutally assaulted and gangraped on 16 December 2012, has impacted the pace of the movement against the death penalty in India. Primacy of life needs to be asserted even against popular and populist outbursts.

IN AN ESSAY written in the *Yale Law Journal* in 1989, scholar Paul Whitlock Cobb Jr. discussed the significance of mercy in the matter of the death penalty. He talked about various facets of compassion. However, he lamented that 'mercy, which encompasses the discretion of decision-makers at every stage of the death penalty process, has been eroded by politics and an increasingly bureaucratized capital punishment system'.[1]

The delay in the execution of the convicts in the 'Nirbhaya' case has led to anguish and dissatisfaction among many people. A plea for mercy was rejected by the President at alarming speed. In the meantime, political parties tried to capitalize on the public sentiment in a blame game with one another, as the Delhi Assembly elections were getting closer.

Aggression on the streets should not replace an informed debate on the death penalty. It is an indubitable fact that what was done to the victim was an extremely heinous crime that warranted severe and meaningful punishment. The grief of Nirbhaya's parents is inestimable. We need to support them even while opposing death penalty.

Empirically, capital punishment has never been an effective remedy against crimes. It does not act as a deterrent. Amidst populist emotions, unpopular views may not be well received. No one will now talk about the age of the accused or their social, educational or economic background. No one will ask if they had any criminal antecedents, or if they are reformable. No one will also dare to talk about the possible innocence of any one among

---

[1] Paul Whitlock Cobb Jr., 'Reviving Mercy in the Structure of Capital Punishment', *The Yale Law Journal*, vol. 99, 1989, p. 389, available at https://digitalcommons.law.yale.edu/cgi/viewcontent.cgi?article=7246&context=ylj, accessed 11 December 2021.

the accused in the crime. If at least one, or more than one, of them had no role in the crime, despite the conviction the state cannot indemnify the life.

American legal scholar Jack Greenberg, in a study, puts the issues in a nutshell: 'The contemporary debate over capital punishment has been conducted principally in terms of whether it is an effective deterrent, appropriately retributive, racially discriminatory, arbitrary, or inevitably prone to error.'[2] The history of the death penalty in India is full of judicial fallacies and constant inconsistencies. A constitution bench of the Supreme Court in *Bachan Singh v. State of Punjab* (1980)[3] authoritatively laid down the law on the topic. The court, after an extensive survey of precedents and global jurisprudence on the topic, said that death penalty is permissible only in the 'rarest of rare cases when the alternative option is unquestionably foreclosed'.

Nirbhaya's murder indisputably belongs to the rarest of rare category. It also shook the conscience of the whole world. The question, however, is whether the alternate option, namely imprisonment for life, is 'unquestionably foreclosed'. Such a discourse requires an ambience of genuine contemplation and deep understanding. The proposition in *Bachan Singh* was not properly applied by several subsequent benches of smaller strength. Though the 'rarest of rare' doctrine was invoked frequently based on the individual notions of judges, examination of whether 'the alternate options are unquestionably foreclosed' was seldom done.

Bachan Singh v. State of Punjab (1980) said that 'judges should never be bloodthirsty' and that 'hanging of murderers has never been too good for them'. More importantly, the constitution bench warned that judges should not be 'oracles or spokesmen of public opinion'. It advocated an accused-centric approach based on the reformability of the individual. But even the Nirbhaya verdict expressly referred to collective conscience as a reason for its conclusions.

The seeming contradictions in the top court's verdicts on the death penalty are curious. In *Santosh Kumar Bariyar v. State of Maharashtra* (2009),[4] a division bench of the court took note of an earlier decision in the *Swamy Shraddananda v. State of Karnataka* (2007)[5] case, in which the court revealed that sentences of death penalty often depended upon 'the personal predilection

---

[2] Jack Greenberg, 'Capital Punishment as a System', *The Yale Law Journal*, vol. 91. no. 5, 1982, pp. 908–36.

[3] (1980) 2 SCC 684.

[4] (2009) 6 SCC 498.

[5] (2007) 12 SCC 288.

of the judges constituting the Bench'. In the *Ravji alias Ram Chandra v. State of Rajasthan* case (1995),[6] the court said that it is the nature of the crime and not factors relating to the accused that are relevant to determine the punishment. This was diametrically opposite to the reformative jurisprudence in *Bachan Singh*. But the erroneous decision in *Ravji* was followed in at least six subsequent cases. The top court was generous enough to acknowledge this serious error in the confessional verdict in *Santosh Kumar Bariyar*. V. Venkatesan, in a 2012 essay, enlisted the names of thirteen convicts who were executed illegally and erroneously.[7]

Curiously, fourteen retired judges wrote a letter to the President in 2012 requesting him to commute the death sentence of thirteen death convicts, as their convictions were erroneous. A bench headed by the then Chief Justice Sathasivam, in January 2014, commuted the death sentence of fifteen convicts. The jurisprudence of death penalty in India thus remains convoluted and complex, and in the process, justice has often become a casualty.

Charles L. Black wrote the book *Capital Punishment: The Inevitability of Caprice and Mistake* way back in 1974. Black highlighted individual and institutional limitations leading to arbitrariness in the decisions on life. No human-made system can ever claim to be fault-free and immaculate. Globally, among the members of the United Nations, more than 135 countries have abolished the death penalty in law or in practice. The preference is for more effective and humane alternatives. As Albert Camus famously said: 'Capital punishment upsets the only indisputable human solidarity – our solidarity against death.'[8]

The New Indian Express, 22 January 2020, https://www.newindianexpress.com/opinions/2020/jan/22/nothing-changes-with-death-penalty-2092789.html

[6] (1996) 2 SCC 175.
[7] V. Venkatesan, 'A Case Against the Death Penalty', *Frontline*, 7 September 2012, available at https://frontline.thehindu.com/cover-story/article30167180.ece, accessed 11 December 2021.
[8] Albert Camus, *Resistance, Rebellion and Death: Essays*, translated by Justin O'Brien, New York: Alfred A. Knopf, 1961.

41. Children, Parents and the Court

Lots of legal reforms are due in the realm of personal laws. We need a different approach in family disputes. This is an area for mediation and conciliation rather than litigation. Shared parenting is a theme that the top court might seriously consider in the near future.

'YOUR CHILDREN ARE not your children. They are the sons and daughters of life's longing for itself', said Kahlil Gibran. The poet went on, 'You may give them your love but not your thoughts, for they have their own thoughts', and warned, 'You may strive to be like them, but seek not to make them like you.' In broken matrimony, Gibran's admonition is hardly honoured.

Children are the primary victims of matrimonial disputes and custody claims. On October 2019, the Supreme Court agreed to examine the possibility of shared parenting for children who undergo the long saga of matrimonial litigation. There are many practical hurdles in implementing the concept in an acute husband–wife skirmish. There is a need for a mass education on the relevance of shared parenting in India. Litigants, lawyers and judges should seriously think about the relevance of a 'parenting plan' in matrimonial litigation, whenever it is necessary or possible. Such an action plan can mitigate the injuries caused to the psyche of children who happen to be in court for no fault on their part.

When spouses are at loggerheads, the fight for 'custody' of the children begins. Indian law generally talks about exclusive custody of children either by the father or the mother, depending upon the age of the children and other circumstances. The phrase 'in the best interest of children' is often given a restricted and partisan meaning. In a few cases, habeas corpus writs are issued by the court asking for production of the child in court, and when such orders are not obeyed, forceful implementation follows. Matrimonial feud denies children the necessary care, affection and protection. In a troubled home, their emotional, ethical and intellectual growth get stalled.

The parental alienation syndrome resulting from exclusive parenting is a serious issue that the court needs to address. On 4 October 2019, a bench of the Supreme Court led by Justice Deepak Gupta reminded family courts about the importance of ensuring visitation right for the parent who is not given regular custody of the child. But even visitation right orders for one of the parents may not be a complete remedy for the pernicious syndrome.

An orthodox legal system treats children as commodities, at least when it comes to custody. This approach is reflected in many custody provisions in the personal laws. For example, the Hindu Minority and Guardianship Act (1956) says that in a valid marriage, the mother will be the custodian till the child attains the age of five years, and thereafter, custody vests with the father. In *Githa Hariharan and Anr. v. The Reserve Bank of India and Anr.* (1999),[1] the Supreme Court tried to balance the custodial claims but the court could not alter the statutory prescription for exclusive custody. Islamic personal law also reflects male domination in the matter. The law governing Christians and Parsis is gender-neutral in this regard, at least textually.

The problem, however, is not only of domination or equality. Broken families are sites of massive violation of the rights of children as well as parents. In *Y. Sulochana Rani v. Union of India*,[2] the Supreme Court agreed to consider the constitutionality of existing personal laws with respect to child custody.

Legal scholar Tamar Ezer observes that 'concepts that are useful in other areas of human rights break down in the context of children', and thus the 'children are an anomaly in the liberal legal order'. She is correct in saying that 'the founders of liberal rights theory perceived children to be outside the scope of their philosophies'.[3] These conceptual limitations are writ large in India's child custody laws.

Section 9 of the Family Courts Act (1984) underlines the need for conciliation and mediation in husband–wife disputes and custody claims. There is a need to develop a different legal culture and professional approach in dealing with family cases. Long litigation in family conflict in itself is inhuman and unwise. Litigation is not always the ultimate method for resolving contrasting interests in a family. Seldom has a judgment satisfied the interests of all the parties to a case as a whole, by balancing their requirements. A family litigation is a different category altogether.

A family court lawyer therefore needs separate training and a different forensic approach, which, unfortunately is not offered by the law colleges or litigation firms in the country. Mediation, not litigation, works as the real solution in many cases. A reconciliatory approach based on a mature understanding and mutual forgiveness can resolve many of the issues.

---

[1] (1999) 2 SCC 228.

[2] WP(C) 903/2019.

[3] Tamar Ezer, 'A Positive Right to Protection for Children', *Yale Human Rights and Development Law Journal*, vol. 7, no. 1, 2004, p. 1, https://papers.ssrn.com/sol3/papers.cfm?abstract_id=3817094, accessed 18 December 2021.

However, there are instances of unilateral abuse and intense exploitation which need stringent judicial remedy.

Maria Montessori correctly said that children become like the things they love. They do not, at any rate, love the hurdles of litigation. Nor do they want to be in a courtroom while being kept away from their classroom or playground. A radical reformation for a child-friendly legal system is the need of the day.

The New Indian Express, 29 November 2020, https://www.newindianexpress.com/opinions/2019/nov/29/matrimonial-disputes-warrant-mass-education-on-shared-parenting-2068596.html.

42. Lakhimpur: A Question of Human Dignity

The law should always be above party politics of the day. However, in the Uttar Pradesh model, the law is only an instrument of the ruling dispensation. In a democracy, it is unthinkable to drive a convoy over a peaceful assembly of protesters. In the Lakhimpur episode in Uttar Pradesh, the power was in clear and direct conflict with the people.

A LOCAL COURT IN Lakhimpur, Uttar Pradesh (U.P.) initially rejected the bail plea of Ashish Mishra, son of Union Minister Ajay Mishra, in the case involving the murder of four farmers and a journalist. Later, though he was released on bail, the Supreme Court cancelled it. A few have been arrested in connection with this incident that happened on 3 October 2021. The allegation is that the farmers and the journalist were killed by a convoy that deliberately ran over them and this was caused by the accused. The video of the scene has shocked our collective conscience. The fact that a few Bharatiya Janata Party (BJP) workers too were killed is equally sad and perturbing. Yet, after the incident, the U.P. Law Minister Brajesh Pathak visited the families of the BJP workers while not caring to meet the families of the farmers who lost their lives.

An elected government and the ministers running it must act in terms of the Constitution, and not merely based on their political beliefs or inclinations. Such an ethical metamorphosis is an imperative, given the letter and spirit of the oath that a minister takes as per the Constitution. Jawaharlal Nehru, on the eve of independence, opined that after the country attains freedom, though there would be a Congress government, it won't be controlled by leaders of the Congress party. This distinction should apply to every dispensation, irrespective of political colour.

However, during a time of democratic crisis this fine division becomes blurred, and the government gets identified with the political party heading it. Worse, even the political parties get reduced to an individual, and the individual is glorified and equalized with the nation. Recall the slogan, 'India is Indira; Indira is India', formulated by D.K. Barooah, a Congress leader, prior to the Emergency (1975–77). At present, political idolatry is re-emerging in the country. It leads to a situation where cabinet ministers act merely as political leaders with partisan interests. This is an indication of democratic degeneration. Tarunabh Khaitan of Oxford University says that right from

2014, the central government 'consistently sought to erase the distinction between the party and the state by incrementally, but systemically, seeking to undermine or capture mechanisms that seek executive accountability'.[1] A reflection of this process, which we also read about in the introduction to this book, is clearly discernible in states like U.P., Assam and Gujarat. A significant impact of this democratic destabilization is clearly manifested in the uprooting of rule of law in such states.

The Lakhimpur incident narrates a changed idea of law enforcement that negates the tenets of constitutionalism. It tells us about much more than mere criminalization of politics. It was in the *Manoj Narula* case (2014)[2] that the Supreme Court said that 'criminalization of politics is an anathema to the sacredness of democracy'. In the judgment, the court emphasized the significance of constitutional morality and good governance. The court said:

> The faith of the people is embedded in the root of the idea of good governance which means reverence for citizenry rights, respect for fundamental rights and statutory rights in any governmental action, deference for unwritten constitutional values, veneration for institutional integrity, and inculcation of accountability to the collective at large.

The Lakhimpur episode, along with several other incidents ranging from Unnao[3] to Hathras,[4] not only shows the increasing crime rate in U.P., but also the regime's attitude towards it. According to a report by the National Crime Records Bureau, U.P. recorded the highest number of murder cases in India (3,779) in 2020. The process of law often takes a back seat here. It required the admonition of the top court even for arresting the accused in the Lakhimpur incident.

---

[1] Tarunabh Khaitan, 'Killing a Constitution with a Thousand Cuts: Executive Aggrandizement and Party-state Fusion in India', *Law and Ethics of Human Rights*, vol. 14, no. 1, https://www.degruyter.com/document/doi/10.1515/lehr-2020-2009/ html accessed 31 December 2021.

[2] See chapter 30.

[3] In Unnao, a 17-year-old girl was gangraped on 4 June 2017. The accused, Kuldeep Singh Sengar, who was a former Member of the Legislative Assembly and a former member of the BJP, was convicted and sentenced to life imprisonment by the court. The girl's father died due to injuries on account of assault. Kuldeep was found guilty for the culpable homicide also.

[4] In Hathras in Uttar Pradesh, on 14 September 2020, a 19-year-old Dalit girl was raped by a gang of upper-caste men. She died two weeks thereafter, due to severe injuries.

It is in the same state that journalists are arrested and incarcerated for doing their job, by invoking draconian laws like the Unlawful Activities (Prevention) Act. Those who protested the Citizenship Amendment Act and the farm laws had to face a similar predicament, as we can recall. False encounter killings and vigilantism have become the new normal. Almost every gathering of people with an agitational gesture was labelled unlawful with Section 144 of the Criminal Procedure Code invoked. Activist Harsh Mander has pointed out that out of 139 persons jailed in 2020 under the National Security Act, 76 were accused of cow slaughter. Alleging 'love jihad', many couples were arrested. The state, which instigated or abetted or justified heinous crimes like murder and rape, was keen to brand personal intimacy a serious offence. Selective use or misuse or non-use of law, in accordance with the temporal requirement of those in power, is the new U.P. brand of justice.

States like Assam and Tripura followed suit. Recall the killing of two people in police firing in Darrang district in Assam. The video of the official photographer thrashing the corpse of a man points to the situation in our troubled times. There is no human dignity without true democracy. As jurist Ronald Dworkin opined, 'equal concern and respect'[5] are the hallmarks of rule of law. Liberty and fraternity are non-negotiable facets of egalitarianism.

In constitutional democracies, rule of law rejects arbitrariness of power, as classically explained by the jurist A.V. Dicey. The law should be always above the politics of the day. However, in the U.P. model, the law is only an instrument of political power. Lakhimpur speaks volumes about the failure of a legal system, and of politics along with it.

The New Indian Express, 18 October 2021, https://www.newindianexpress.com/opinions/columns/2021/oct/19/lakhimpur-a-question-of-human-dignity-2372896.html

---

[5] Ronald Dworkin, *Taking Rights Seriously*, London: Duckworth, 1977.

43. AFSPA: A Law Warranting Immediate Repeal

The Armed Forces Special Powers Act (AFSPA), 1958 has a pernicious effect on human lives in India. The pity is that the statute as well as the forces that were designed for the people of the country, unreasonably and unjustly burden them instead. It is shocking that even after the massacre in Nagaland in the first week of December 2021, the centre does not genuinely introspect. On 30 December 2021, it extended AFSPA in the state for another six months.[1] Paradoxically, a high-level committee was also constituted to look into the question of repeal of the enactment in the area.[2] The Act is now withdrawn only from parts of some North East states. The Supreme Court had validated the enactment in Naga People's Movement of Human Rights v. Union of India (1998).[3] *But this validation is not a reason for continuation of the enactment, said the report of the Jeevan Reddy Committee (2005),[4] constituted to review the enactment. This article pleads for the implementation of the report.*

THE TRAGEDY IN Nagaland is deeply disturbing. On 4 December 2021, in a botched army ambush, fourteen civilians and a soldier were killed. On the face of it, it was gross intelligence failure. An egregious error in judgement led to the killing of innocents. The executive excess had a devastating effect, given the irrational immunity provided by the law. The commando unit was instigated and abetted, at least indirectly, by the Armed Forces (Special Powers) Act (AFSPA), 1958, in which lawlessness becomes the law. Such incidents are a culmination of the impunity granted to the army by the statute. It is unfortunate that the incident might adversely impact the progress that the country has made in the discourse with armed rebels in the North East.

---

[1] 'AFSPA Extended in Nagaland for 6 Months with Effect from Today', *Mint*, 30 December 2021, https://www.livemint.com/news/india/afspa-extended-in-nagaland-for-6-months-with-effect-from-today-11640834754250.html, accessed 1 January 2022.

[2] Ibid.

[3] (1998) 2 SCC 109.

[4] Report of the Committee to Review the Armed Forces (Special Powers) Act, 1958, Ministry of Home Affairs, Government of India, 2005, https://andyreiter.com/wp-content/uploads/military-justice/in/Government%20Documents/India%20-%202005%20-%20Report%20of%20the%20Committee%20to%20Review%20AFSPA%20(Reddy%20Report).pdf, accessed 1 January 2022.

The law had a paradoxical origin, and an equally paradoxical evolution. The British designed it by way of an ordinance in 1942 as a device to suppress the Quit India movement; post-Independence, the Parliament enacted it on 11 September 1958. Pandit Nehru justified it as an essential legal tool against those who try to 'coerce the governmental authority by organized violence'.

But the history of the law also unfolds the history of crimes committed by the army on India's people. Those were often crimes without punishment. In 1995, a convoy of the Rashtriya Rifles with hundreds of jawans fired at civilians in Kohima city. Seven people were killed and many injured. In 2000, in the Malom massacre, Manipur, ten civilians were allegedly shot down by a unit of the Assam Rifles. Irom Sharmila's hunger strike began to protest against this brutality, which then developed into a crusade against the law as such. In 2004, in Manipur, a woman was raped and murdered, and men of the Assam Rifles were accused of committing the heinous crime. This led to an unprecedented agitation in which the women expressed their anger and anguish all in one banner, saying 'Indian Army, Rape Us'.

As such, the law has not been safe in the hands of the Assam Rifles, and an indication to the contrary in a recent article[5] is contestable. The Assam Rifles has a curious origin. It was devised by the British to fight tribes in the North East that raised their voice against the Raj. Strangely, as in the case of AFSPA, this force too was retained by the government to fight rebels against the sovereign. Power often speaks the same language. The pity is that the statute as well as forces designed for the people of the country unreasonably and unjustly burden them instead. Extra-Judicial Execution Victim Families Association Manipur (EEVFAM), an organization formed by victims of army atrocities, alleges that thousands have been killed in fake encounters over the last few decades in AFSPA-operated areas. Insurgency always arms the state, and between the insurgent and the state, the rights of citizens get crushed.

The statute has arbitrary contents. For example, Section 3 gives power to the government to declare certain parts of the country as 'disturbed areas', and Section 4 allows an officer of the armed forces to 'fire upon or otherwise use force, even to the causing of death', against persons breaking the law or lawful orders, as per the conditions stated in the Act. This power is meant to be used for 'the maintenance of public order'. The Section also empowers the army to

[5] Pradip Phanjoubam, 'Nagaland Ambush Reopens Old AFSPA Wound in Northeast', *The New Indian Express*, 10 December 2021, https://www.newindianexpress.com/opinions/2021/dec/10/nagaland-ambush-reopens-old-afspa-wound-in-northeast-2393778.html, accessed 10 December 2021.

arrest persons, enter premises and conduct search and seizure without a warrant from any authority. By virtue of Section 6, protection is granted to 'persons acting under (the) Act'. The statute does not even require that the acts, to qualify for protection, should be done in good faith, a rider that the law adopts in several other enactments. The cumulative effect of these provisions creates a kind of military regime in the AFSPA-declared areas. This makes a mockery of the right to life guaranteed by Article 21 of the Indian Constitution.

The Act applies only on declaration that a state or part of it is a 'disturbed area'. Thus the law is selective in its application, resulting in blatant geographical discrimination. The tenure of the law is often extended mechanically. At present, the Act applies to Assam, Nagaland, and a good part of Manipur and Arunachal Pradesh, apart from Jammu and Kashmir, where a separate law was enacted in 1990 with almost the same content.

In *Extra-Judicial Execution Victim Families Association v. Union of India* (2016),[6] the Supreme Court said that the statute does not provide a 'blanket immunity' to the perpetrators if the action is unjustified. The court prescribed a thorough enquiry into 'each instance of an alleged extra-judicial killing'. But the fact of the matter is that complaints by individuals and even first information reports registered by the state police are either discarded or simply vanish. Though the apex court ruling has precedential value in the context of pleas for probe or compensation, it is inadequate to prevent crimes committed under the guise of law enforcement. What is more relevant is the Jeevan Reddy Committee Report, which takes into account the social, political and other related aspects of the matter. After a comprehensive study, the Committee said: '[The AFSPA] should be repealed. Therefore, recommending the continuation of the present Act, with or without amendments, does not arise. The Act is too sketchy, too bald and quite inadequate in several particulars.'[7]

Democracy, after all, is a perpetual process of course correction. Mere state actions and decisions without a genuine concern for human rights will not resolve the issue. Technological advancement in recent times also makes the logic of the 1958 statute obsolete. So also, AFSPA needs to be scrapped altogether. In doing so, the state will only be trying to heal the wounds that the law has mercilessly inflicted on the nation.

The New Indian Express, 14 December 2021, https://www.newindianexpress.com/opinions/columns/2021/dec/14/afspa-a-law-warranting-immediate-repeal-2395151.html.

---

[6] (2016) 14 SCC 536.
[7] Jeevan Reddy Committee Report, 2005.

Conclusion: Constitution as a Political Tool

SINCE 2014, OUR constitutional heritage has suffered significant damage, which got aggravated when the concerns in this work were raised (2018–21). The political transformation in India has challenged the basic foundations of the nation. The Hindutva ideology, supported by the cadre organization Rashtriya Swayamsevak Sangh (RSS) and associated outfits, is essentially antithetical to the constitutional values of a liberal democracy.

The ideological and organizational character of the new regime created a scenario radically different from that during the National Emergency proclaimed by Indira Gandhi on 25 June 1975. During the Emergency, there was consolidation of opposition and civil rights organizations beyond religious, doctrinal or even political lines. Even the Jan Sangh was part of the political opposition, despite its brazen Hindutva agenda.

On the other hand, at present, the regime has been able to divide the society not only on communal and religious lines, but on political lines as well. An atmosphere of hatred and fear is deliberately created as a part of its political strategy. For the ruling front, the Constitution has been a means to capture power; and having acquired power using the Constitution's own apparatus, the next move was to revitalize the 100-year-old Hindutva project which, in its political praxis, always negated the democratic Constitution. No wonder that after the notorious Haridwar hate speech in December 2021 calling for genocide of the Muslims, Yati Narsinghanand, a leader of the Dharam Sansad reportedly said: 'We have no trust in the Supreme Court and the Constitution.'[1] The new normal of vigilantism and divisive strategies is interlinked with concrete state power.

When it comes to the economic front, ironically, the state policy consistently aligns with the modern-day capitalists, and that too, in a very selective manner. The national assets are assigned to preferred tycoons. Policies are often designed and implemented vigorously so as to benefit these privileged few with scant regard to the public interest or the socialist pointers in the Constitution. Both structurally and functionally, we are almost a theocratic state with a clear affinity towards the capitalist monopolies. Hate

---

[1] 'We Have No Faith in Supreme Court and Constitution, says Yati Narsinghanand Giri', *Scroll.in*, 14 January 2022, https://scroll.in/video/1015045/watch-we-have-no-faith-in-supreme-court-and-constitution-says-yati-narsinghanand-giri, accessed 18 January 2022.

as an ideology has replaced communitarian values. The picture of an assembly of Hindu villagers in Chhattisgarh taking an oath 'to boycott the Muslims' appeared widely in the media. The *hijab* ban in Karnataka facilitated by the state government also had a divisive agenda. As Christophe Jaffrelot noted, the country is 'transitioning from a de facto Hindu Rashtra to an authoritarian Hindu Raj (Hindu nation-state)'.[2]

But unlike what happened during the National Emergency, there is no slum demolition, or compulsory and abusive sterilization, or blunt censorship, or massive arrest of opposition leaders, even under the Modi-2 dispensation. Institutional damage happens only in a gradual and obscure manner with an outward appearance of a working democracy where elections take place almost regularly and institutions somehow function. With a huge propaganda machine, the right-wing Hindutva brigade ultimately manages the voters 'tactically' and often 'successfully'. The central government also slowly manifests into an autocracy rooted in idolatry, about which Dr Ambedkar repeatedly warned.

Significantly, those in power try to woo a good section of the people even by deceptive means, and thereby mass support is created for a system under a demagogue. The media, including the social media, are effectively and easily used in this strategy by the Bharatiya Janata Party (BJP) and the union government, which are incredibly rich and powerful, so as to purchase, hire, manipulate or control the content of conversations both online and offline. We are not just a democracy in crisis. We are almost in a state of 'despotism' where 'democide' has begun already, as convincingly demonstrated by Debasish Roy Chowdhury and John Keane in their recent work.[3] As they point out, there is an erosion in the social foundations of democracy as reflected in innumerable issues faced by people, like poverty, lack of access to resources, mounting disparity, absence of health care and educational and travel facilities, unemployment, environmental degradation, etc.[4] Crony capitalism in India is monstrous in its form, blatant in its actions and brutal in its effect.

Aakar Patel, in his seminal work *Price of the Modi Years*, explains how governance in India has suffered in the recent past. On almost every front,

---

[2] Christophe Jaffrelot, *Modi's India: Hindu Nationalism and the Rise of Ethnic Democracy*, Princeton, NJ: Princeton University Press, 2021.

[3] Debasish Roy Chowdhury and John Keane, *To Kill a Democracy: India's Passage to Despotism*, New Delhi: Macmillan, 2021.

[4] Ibid.

the government has failed. The economy has been shattered, and democratic spaces in private and public lives have shrunk enormously. The country's happiness level has fallen drastically. Patel writes that 'Modi's popularity does not come from his performance' but 'from his divisiveness and his hard majoritarianism'. He adds that 'India has become less resistant to the poison, with its institutional capacity weakened, its media made rabid and society polarized and perpetually on edge'.[5]

Let us turn to the Constitution. Chanchal Kumar Singh rightly noted that 'more than two-thirds provisions of the Constitution relate to governance'.[6] In a 1992 paper, Amir Arjomand wrote: 'Constitutions are important social realities in the contemporary world, whether in force or in suspense. They are important as transcendental justifications of political order. When suspended or breached in practice, as is often the case, they delegitimize governments and constitute normative assets for the opposition.'[7]

This can however happen in normal situations of suspending or breaching the Constitution, and when the political opposition consolidates over the foundations of the basic law. In contemporary India, the effort should be to strengthen the very foundation of the Constitution, as the state has been overtly and covertly damaging it.

The essential nexus between deconstitutionalization and the collapse of the idea of good governance is evident. The Hindutva ideology, which lacks any egalitarian plan for a complex nation like India, is bound to fail. Indian majoritarianism, with its hollow rhetoric, is inherently incapable of fulfilling the constitutional aspirations. It is bothersome that the failure of the opposition in India lies in its inability not only to consolidate politically, but to formulate a strategy of governance at the state and central levels.

Along with the fundamental rights, let us also re-read the Directive Principles of State Policy contained in Part IV of the country's basic law, which is a manifesto for a just, peaceful and fair socio-economic structure. We have examined this aspect in different contexts in some of the earlier chapters.[8] Part IV of the Constitution enumerates the strategies for a social order rooted

---

[5] Aakar Patel, *Price of the Modi Years*, Chennai: Westland, 2021.

[6] Chanchal Kumar Singh, 'Economic Policies and Political Processes in the Pursuit of Constitutional Goals', *Journal of Indian Law Institute*, vol. 53, no. 2, April–June 2011, pp. 333–35.

[7] Saïd Amir Arjomand, 'Constitutions and the Struggle for Political Order: A Study in the Modernization of Political Traditions', *European Journal of Sociology*, vol. 33, no. 1, 1992, pp. 39–82

[8] See chapters 26, 27 and 36 of this book.

in people's welfare. It wants the state 'to eliminate inequalities in status, facilities, and opportunities, not only amongst individuals but also amongst groups of people residing in different areas or engaged in different vocations'.[9] By way of different articles, Part IV persuades the state to ensure 'adequate means of livelihood'[10] and distribution of 'ownership and control of the material resources of the community' so as to 'subserve the common good'.[11] It demands that the state ensure a system where there is no 'concentration of wealth and means of production to the common detriment'.[12] It talks about equal pay for equal work,[13] living wages,[14] child care,[15] healthy development of children,[16] decentralization of power,[17] right to education,[18] workers' participation in management,[19] nutrition,[20] public health,[21] agricultural activities,[22] environmental protection,[23] etc. As per Article 37, the Directive Principles are not enforceable by any court. The point, however, is that these principles are politically enforceable. For that, constitutional wisdom needs to be a part of people's lives. It must be an empirical reality for the masses. It must be the country's experience. A federal opposition to the central dispensation based on real issues of the people is vital. Federalism is synonymous with pluralism. It embodies inclusiveness. It involves decentralization of power. It is the surest safeguard against centralizing rabble-rousers.

The propaganda that the Constitution of India as such is 'western' needs to be exposed. The basic tenets of the fundamental law, like equality, liberty or fraternity, have indigenous traits in Buddhism and in certain rare streams of Hinduism. Even otherwise, (western) liberalism has many intrinsic and empirical virtues, which enormously helped in emancipating the marginalized and the downtrodden in India. True, that we could not achieve all the goals.

[9] Article 38(2) of the Constitution of India.
[10] Article 39(a).
[11] Article 39(b).
[12] Article 39(c).
[13] Article 39(d).
[14] Article 43.
[15] Article 45.
[16] Article 39(e), (f) and Article 45.
[17] Article 40.
[18] Article 41.
[19] Article 43A.
[20] Article 47.
[21] Article 47.
[22] Article 48.
[23] Article 48A.

But without a politics based at least feebly on a democratic legal framework, the situation would have been worse.

It is also essential to recognize the universality of constitutionalism in the contemporary world. Modernism and modernity are civilizational imperatives. So is the case with secularism. Democracy contains a set of core values connected with one another. Populist autocracies in other countries like Russia, Brazil, Poland, Hungary, Ecuador, Philippines and Venezuela are a sad commentary on the decline of the universal principles of democracy, people's rights and human dignity.

Let us see it as it is: the Sangh Parivar politics in India is essentially undemocratic, dishonest and deceptive. It is anti-national in the constitutional sense. The political struggle in India is between those who stand by the country's Constitution and those who reject it. This is the message the chapters in this book try to convey. The Constitution is the only political tool that the nation can effectively use to revive and improve her democracy. The last four years have, in curious ways, emphasized the indispensability of the foundational values of the Republic. Consolidated mass action in India, as we could see in the people's movement against the farm laws and the Citizenship Amendment Act, demonstrates this reality. It is for the political opposition and other societal groups to carry the task forward.

The Constitution always needs a language with which to connect to the people and its institutions. It needs a pedagogical process capable of maintaining itself and developing its doctrinal precepts into mass movements during challenging times. India's poverty, inequality and illiteracy have been the main obstacles in invoking the hidden energy in the fundamental law as a means of political emancipation. We also need to address issues like communal violence, the growing criminalization of politics, and the conversion of elections to a mere farce regulated by big money and muscle power. Constitutionalism can thrive only with the idea of egalitarianism. Viewed this way, we have not been able to constitutionalize our polity in the true and full sense of the term. This is an area where we have failed as a nation. This, again, is the realization with which we can succeed as a nation.

GPSR Authorized Representative: Easy Access System Europe, Mustamäe tee
50, 10621 Tallinn, Estonia, gpsr.requests@easproject.com

www.ingramcontent.com/pod-product-compliance
Lightning Source LLC
Chambersburg PA
CBHW051729260326
41914CB00040B/2032/J

9 7 8 8 1 9 5 0 5 5 9 8 2